EMOTIONALLY HEALTHY SPIRITUALITY

EMOTIONALLY HEALTHY SPIRITUALITY

UNLEASH A REVOLUTION IN YOUR LIFE IN CHRIST

PETER SCAZZERO

THOMAS NELSON
Since 1798

NASHVILLE DALLAS MEXICO CITY RIO DE JANEIRO BEIJING

Emotionally Healthy Spirituality

Published in Nashville, Tennessee, by Thomas Nelson. Thomas Nelson is a trademark of Thomas Nelson, Inc.

Thomas Nelson, Inc. titles may be purchased in bulk for educational, business, fund-raising, or sales promotional use. For information, please e-mail SpecialMarkets@thomasnelson.com.

Cover Design: Christopher Tobias, Tobias' Outerwear for Books
Cover Photo: Getty Images and PixelWorks Studios, www.shootpw.com
Interior Design: Sharon Collins/Artichoke Design

Library of Congress Cataloging-in-Publication Data

Scazzero, Peter, 1956-
Emotionally healthy spirituality : unleash a revolution in your life in Christ / Peter Scazzero.
p. cm.
Summary: "Help to experience a faith charged with authenticity, contemplation, and a hunger for God"—Provided by publisher.
ISBN-13: 978-1-59145-452-6 (hardcover)
ISBN-10: 1-59145-452-2 (hardcover)
1. Spirituality. 2. Spiritual formation. 3. Religious addiction. I. Title.
BV4501.3.S29 2006
248.4—dc22

2006013039

Printed in the United States of America
07 08 09 10 11 QW 11 10 9 8 7 6 5

CONTENTS

ACKNOWLEDGMENTS

Although this book was written by me, the material was birthed with Geri, my best friend and wife for the last twenty-two years. We have lived the insights of this book separately, as a married couple, and as parents of our four girls—Maria, Christy, Faith, and Eva.

I would like to thank the family of New Life Fellowship Church in Queens, New York City, where I have been senior pastor for the last nineteen years. This book was written out of the reality of our life together as a multiracial, multiethnic community committed to bridging racial, cultural, economic, and gender barriers, and to serving the poor and marginalized. The content of this book emerged out of this soil; their openness to the Holy Spirit and passion for the Lord Jesus is a gift. I want to express specific appreciation to the elders, staff, leaders, members, and close friends of New Life, and to all those who read drafts and portions of this book along the way (there are too many to mention by name). Thank you all.

I want to thank Peter Schreck of Palmer Theological Seminary, along with Chris Giammona, Emma Baez, Peter Hoffman, and Jay Feld. Each read critical chapters and made significant contributions over time. Thank you to Mike Favilla for his many hours of work on early drafts of the illustrations found in the book. Thank you to Kathy Helmers, my agent, who has been a gift and a guide through the entire process. Thanks to Joey Paul and Kris Bearss, publishers at Integrity, who through their perceptive questions and insights took this book to another level. Thanks also to Leslie Peterson, my editor, for her excellent work, along with the many other people who brought this manuscript to publication.

INTRODUCTION

This book is not meant to merely provide information. It is meant to change your life. It is an invitation to a deeper and wider relationship with Jesus Christ, requiring you to journey into the unknown, much like Abraham did when he left his comfortable home in Ur. The combination of emotional health and contemplative spirituality—the heart of the message found on these pages—will unleash a revolution into the deep places of your life. This revolution will, in turn, transform all your relationships.

In 2003 I wrote a book for church leaders and pastors entitled *The Emotionally Healthy Church*.[1] The impact of this book surprised us, and we recognized that God truly had given us some insights into how to bring emotional health and spirituality together. It dramatically changed our lives and many others' at New Life Fellowship Church in Queens, New York City. Once we began to travel and offer seminars, we realized the extent to which the first book touched an exposed nerve among leaders and pastors across all denominational and theological lines. The message of the book spread rapidly across North America and overseas.

This book is distinct in three very important ways. First I wanted to make available the life-changing material we developed in *The Emotionally Healthy Church* not just to pastors and leaders but to the average church attender. Second, for those of you who read the first book, you will notice other principles have been added, reworked, and sharpened. The last four years have provided rich time for reflection and discussion around this material. Finally, I write with a burning passion to make the ancient treasures of the church accessible as well. The contemplative tradition has brought a fullness, a richness, and a sense of wholeness to our disciple making and spiritual formation at New Life Fellowship Church. The result has been nothing short of explosive (I do not know what other word to use!) in the lives of many people.

I have been senior pastor at New Life Fellowship for nineteen years. People from over sixty-five nations stream through our doors each week. This has provided a unique window for working this material into a local church family. It has been an exhilarating experience. As a church community we have been slowly absorbing the principles found in this book for over ten years. Each subject found in the different chapters has been pondered on, preached on, prayed for, applied, and lived out by members of our church (and myself). Little by little, they took it in for their own journey with Christ.

Now it is your turn. So please read this book prayerfully . . . thoughtfully . . . slowly. Stop to absorb the glimpses of God and yourself that the Holy Spirit gives you along the way. Write down how God speaks to you. When I read an edifying book where God is coming to me, I write inside the back cover a few sentences about each insight along with the page number. This way I can go back later and easily review what God said to me. You may want to journal or write in the margins of this book.

Pray the prayers, slowly, at the end of each chapter. Don't hurry. Each chapter could easily have been expanded to be its own book. There is a lot to chew on here.

Most importantly, savor and cherish the Lord Jesus Christ as you meet him in these pages. You want to grow in your experience of Jesus, not merely add to your head knowledge about him.

The book is divided up simply. The first section is entitled "Emotionally Unhealthy Spirituality." These chapters are intended to help you recognize the nature of what an emotionally *un*healthy spirituality looks like. It is important you clearly see the nature and scope of the problem before reading about the radical and far-reaching antidote. Chapter three provides the hinge upon which the rest of the book turns, explaining why both emotional health and contemplative spirituality are indispensable to bringing transformation in Christ to the deep places of our lives. You may want to return to reread that chapter when you finish the book. Section two of the book, chapters four through ten, then addresses the specific pathways essential to developing an emotionally healthy spirituality.

John of the Cross, in the introduction to his book *The Living Flame*, noted that everything he wrote was "as far from the reality as is a painting from the living object represented."[2] Nonetheless, he ventured to write what he did know. In the same way, this book cannot capture the incomprehensible and inexhaustible God we seek to know and to love. We will spend eternity getting to know him better. Remember as you read that these words also are like a painting, directing us to a richer, more authentic encounter with the living God in Christ. The real success of this book will be measured by a positive change in your relationship to Jesus, yourself, and others.

Since a lack of emotional health early in my ministry almost caused me to crash, I am thankful to God for his mercy. This has enabled me to not only survive but to enjoy a richness of the Christian life that I never imagined. If you are hungry for God to transform both you and those around you, I invite you to turn the page and begin reading.

PART ONE

THE PROBLEM OF EMOTIONALLY UNHEALTHY SPIRITUALITY

CHAPTER ONE

RECOGNIZING TIP-OF-THE-ICEBERG SPIRITUALITY

Something Is Desperately Wrong

Christian spirituality, without an integration of emotional health, can be deadly—to yourself, your relationship with God, and the people around you. I know. Having lived half my adult life this way, I have more personal illustrations than I care to recount.

The following is one I wish I could forget.

FAITH AND THE POOL

I met John and Susan while speaking at another church. They were excited and enthusiastic about visiting New Life Fellowship Church in Queens where I pastor. On a hot, humid July Sunday, they made the long, arduous drive from Connecticut, with all the predictable traffic, to sit through our three services. Between the second and third service John pulled me aside to let me know they hoped to get some time to talk with Geri and me.

I was exhausted. But my greater concern was what their pastor, a friend of mine, would think. What would they say to him if I simply sent them home? What might they say about me?

So I lied.

"Sure, I would love to have you for a late-afternoon lunch. I'm sure Geri would too!"

Geri, in her desire to be a "good pastor's wife," agreed to the lunch when I called, even though she, too, would have preferred to say no. John, Susan, and I arrived home about three o'clock in the afternoon. Within a few minutes, the four of us sat down to eat.

Then John began to talk . . . and talk . . . and talk. . . . Susan said nothing.

Geri and I would occasionally glance at each other. We felt we had to give him time. But how much?

John continued to talk . . . and talk . . . and talk. . . .

I couldn't interrupt him. He was sharing with such intensity about God, his life, his new opportunities at work. *Oh God, I want to be loving and kind, but how much is enough?* I wondered to myself as I pretended to listen. I was angry. Then I felt guilty about my anger. I wanted John and Susan to think of Geri and me as hospitable and gracious. Why didn't he give his wife a chance to say something? Or us?

Finally, Susan took a bathroom break. John excused himself to make a quick phone call. Geri spoke up once we were alone.

"Pete, I can't believe you did this!" she mumbled in an annoyed voice. "I haven't seen you. The kids haven't seen you."

I put my head down and slumped my shoulders, hoping my humility before her would evoke mercy.

It didn't.

Susan returned from the bathroom and John continued talking. I hated sitting at that kitchen table.

"I hope I'm not talking too much," John said unsuspectingly.

"No, of course not." I continued to lie on our behalf. I assured him, "It's great having you here."

Geri was silent next to me. I did not want to look over.

After another hour, Geri blurted out during a rare pause, "I haven't heard from Faith in a while." Faith was our three-year-old daughter.

John continued talking as if Geri hadn't said a word. Geri and I exchanged glances again and continued pretending to listen, occasionally stretching our necks to look outside the room.

Oh, I'm sure everything is all right, I convinced myself.

Geri, however, began to look very upset. Her face revealed tension, worry, and impatience. I could tell her mind was racing through options of where Faith might be.

The house was way too quiet.

John continued talking.

Finally, Geri excused herself with what I could tell was an annoyed tone: "I have to go and check on our daughter."

She darted down to the basement. No Faith. The bedrooms. No Faith. The living and dining rooms. No Faith.

Frantically, she ran back into the kitchen. "Pete! Oh my God, I can't find her. She's not here!"

Horror gripped us both as our eyes locked for a nanosecond. We were both pondering the unthinkable: the pool!

Despite the fact that we lived in a two-family, semi-attached house with little space, we did have a small three-foot-high pool in our backyard for relief from the hot New York City summers. We ran to the backyard . . . and saw our worst fears realized.

There stood Faith in the middle of the pool with her back to us—our three-year-old daughter, naked, barely standing on tiptoes with water up to her chin, almost in her mouth.

At that moment I felt us age five years.

"Faith. Don't move!" Geri yelled as we ran to pull her out of the pool.

Somehow Faith had let herself up and down the ladder into the water without slipping. And she had kept herself standing on her tiptoes in the pool for who knows how long!

If she had faltered, Geri and I would have been burying our daughter.

Geri and I were badly shaken—for days. I shudder even today as I write these words.

The sad truth about this incident is that nothing changed inside us. That would take five more years, a lot more pain, and a few more close calls.

How could I, along with Geri, have been so negligent? I look back in embarrassment at how untruthful and immature I acted with John and Susan, with God, with myself! John wasn't the problem; I was. Externally I had appeared kind, gracious, and patient, when inwardly I was nothing like that. I so wanted to present a polished image as a good Christian that I cut myself off from what was going on within myself. Unconsciously I had been thinking: *I hope I am a good-enough Christian. Will this couple like us? Will they think we are okay? Will John give a good report of his visit to my pastor friend?*

Pretending was safer than honesty and vulnerability.

The reality was that my discipleship and spirituality had not touched a number of deep internal wounds and sin patterns—especially those ugly ones that emerged behind the closed doors of our home during trials, disagreements, conflicts, and setbacks.

I was stuck at an immature level of spiritual and emotional development. And my then-present way of living the Christian life was not transforming the deep places in my life.

And because of that, Faith almost died. Something was dreadfully wrong with my spirituality—but what?

CHURCH LEAVERS

Researchers have been charting the departing dust of those known as "church leavers"[1]—an increasingly large group that has been gathering numbers in recent years. Some of these leavers are believers who no longer attend church. These men and women made a genuine commitment to Christ but came to realize, slowly and painfully, that the spirituality available in church had not really delivered any deep, Christ-transforming life change—either in themselves or others.

What went wrong? They were sincere followers of Jesus Christ, but they struggled as much as anyone else with their marriages, divorces, friendships, parenting, singleness, sexuality, addictions, insecurities, drive for approval, and feelings of failure and depression at work, church, and home. They saw the same patterns of emotional conflict inside the church as outside. What was wrong with the church?

Other church leavers include those who remained in the church but simply became inactive. After many years of frustration and disappointment, realizing that the black-and-white presentations of the life of faith did not fit with their life experience, they quit—at least internally. For the sake of their children, or perhaps for lack of an alternative, they have remained in the church, but passively. They can't quite put their finger on the problem, but they know something is not right. Something is missing. A deep unease in their soul gnaws at them, but they don't know what to do about it.

A third group, sadly, chose to jettison their faith completely. They grew tired of feeling stuck and trapped in their spiritual journey. And they grew weary of Christians around them who, regardless of their "knowledge" of God, church involvement, and zeal, were angry, compulsive, highly opinionated, defensive, proud, and too busy to love the Jesus they professed. Being a Christian seemed more trouble than it was worth. Starbucks and the *New York Times* were better companions for Sunday mornings.

There was a time in my life when I wanted more than anything else to be one of those church leavers. The agonizing pain of a major crisis had me writhing in anger and shame—*me*, the guy who had tried so hard to be a committed and loving Christian, who was so sincere about serving God and his kingdom. How had all my best efforts landed me in such a mess?

It wasn't until the pain exposed how much was hiding under my surface of being a "good Christian" that it hit me: whole layers of my emotional life had lain buried, untouched by God's transforming power. I had been too busy for "morbid introspection," too consumed with building God's work to spend time digging around in my subconscious. Yet now the pain was forcing me to face how superficially Jesus had penetrated my inner person, even though I had been a Christian for twenty years.

That is when I discovered the radical truth that changed my life, my marriage, my ministry, and eventually the church we were privileged to serve. It was a simple truth, but somehow I'd missed it—and, strangely, apparently so had the vast majority of the evangelical movement I'd been part of. This simple but profound reality, I believe, has the power to bring revolutionary change to many of those who are ready to throw in the towel on Christian faith: emotional health and spiritual maturity are inseparable.

GROWING UP EMOTIONALLY UNDEVELOPED

Very, very few people emerge out of their families of origin emotionally whole or mature. In my early years of ministry, I believed the power of Christ could break any curse, so I barely gave any thought to how the home I'd left long ago might still be shaping me. After all, didn't Paul teach in 2 Corinthians 5:17 that when you become a Christian, old things pass away and all things become new? But crisis taught me I had to go back and understand what those old things were in order for them to begin passing away.

My Italian-American family, like all families, was cracked and broken. My parents were children of immigrants and sacrificed themselves for their four children to enjoy the American dream. My dad, a baker by trade, worked endless hours, first in a New York City Italian pastry shop owned by my grandfather and later for a large baking distributor. His one overriding goal was for his children to study, graduate from college, and "make something of their lives."

My mom struggled with clinical depression and an emotionally unavailable husband. Raised under an abusive father, she suffocated under the weight of raising her four children alone. Her married life, like her childhood, was marked by sadness and loneliness.

My siblings and I emerged out of that environment scarred. We were emotionally underdeveloped and starved for affection and attention. We each left home for college, trying unsuccessfully not to look back.

From the outside our home, like so many others, appeared okay. It seemed better, at least, than most of my friends' situations. The house of cards, however, came tumbling down when I was sixteen. My older brother broke an invisible rule of our family by disobeying my father and quitting college. Even worse, he announced that Reverend and Mrs. Moon, founders of the Unification Church, were the true parents of humankind. For the next ten years he was declared dead and forbidden to return home. My parents were ashamed and crushed. They drew back from extended family and friends. The pressure and stress of his dramatic leaving exposed the large craters and holes in our family functioning. We splintered further apart.

It would take us almost two decades to begin recovering.

What is perhaps most tragic is that my dad's spirituality and loyal involvement in his church (he was the one member of our family with any spark of genuine faith) had little impact on his marriage and parenting. The way he functioned as a father, husband, and employee reflected his culture and family of origin rather than the new family of Jesus.

My family is undoubtedly different from yours. But one thing I've learned after over twenty years of working closely with families is this: your family, like mine, is also marked by the consequences of the disobedience of our first parents as described in Genesis 3. Shame, secrets, lies, betrayals, relationship breakdowns, disappointments, and unresolved longings for unconditional love lie beneath the veneer of even the most respectable families.

COMING TO FAITH IN CHRIST

Disillusioned and unsure of God's existence, by the age of thirteen I had left the church, convinced it was irrelevant to "real life." It was through a Christian concert in a small church and a Bible study on our university campus that, by God's grace, I became a Christian. I was nineteen. The enormousness of the love of God in Christ overwhelmed me. I immediately began a passionate quest to know this living Jesus who had revealed himself to me.

For the next seventeen years, I plunged headfirst into my newfound evangelical/charismatic tradition, absorbing every drop of discipleship and spirituality made available. I prayed and read Scripture. I consumed Christian books. I participated in small groups and attended church regularly. I learned about spiritual disciplines. I served eagerly with my gifts. I gave money away freely. I shared my faith with anyone who would listen.

Following college graduation, I taught high school English for one year and then went to work for three years as a staff person with InterVarsity Christian Fellowship, a Christian ministry serving college students. Eventually this led me to Princeton and Gordon-Conwell Theological Seminaries, one year in Costa Rica to learn Spanish, and the planting of a multiethnic church in Queens, New York.

For those first seventeen years as a devoted follower of Christ, however, the emotional aspects or areas of my humanity remained largely untouched. They were rarely talked about or touched on in Sunday school classes, small groups, or church settings. In fact, the phrase "emotional aspects or areas of my humanity" seemed to belong in a professional counselor's vocabulary, not the church.

TRYING DIFFERENT APPROACHES TO DISCIPLESHIP

Just as my leadership ministry seemed to be reaching full swing, Geri, my wife, slowly began to protest that something was desperately wrong—wrong with me and wrong with the church. I knew she might be right so I kept trying to implement different discipleship emphases that, to a certain degree, helped me. My conversation with myself went something like this:

"More Bible study, Pete. That will change people. Their minds will be renewed. Changed lives will follow."

"No. It is body life. Get everyone in deeper levels of community, in small groups. That will do it!"

"Pete, remember, deep change requires the power of the Spirit. That can only come through prayer. Spend more time in prayer yourself and schedule more prayer meetings at New Life. God doesn't move unless we pray."

"No, these are spiritual warfare issues. The reason people aren't really changing is you are not confronting the demonic powers in and around them. Apply Scripture and pray in Jesus' authority for people to be set free from the evil one."

"Worship. That's it. If people will only soak in the presence of God in worship, that will work."

"Remember Christ's words from Matthew 25:40. We meet Christ when we give freely to 'the least of these brothers of mine,' those sick, unknown, in prison. Get them involved in serving among the poor; they will change."

"No, Pete, you need people who hear God in an exceptional way and have prophetic insight. They will finally break the unseen chains around people."

"Enough, Pete. People don't really understand the grace of God in the gospel. Our standing before God is based on Jesus' record and performance, not our own. It is his righteousness, not ours! Pound it into their heads every day, as Luther said, and they'll change!"

There is biblical truth in each of these points. I believe all of them have a place in our spiritual journey and development. You, no doubt, have experienced God and his presence through one or more of these in your walk with Christ.

The problem, however, is that inevitably you find, as I did, something is still missing. In fact, the spirituality of most current discipleship models often only adds an additional protective layer against people growing up emotionally. Because people are having real, and helpful, spiritual experiences in certain areas of their lives—such as worship, prayer, Bible studies, and fellowship—they mistakenly believe they are doing fine, even if their relational life and interior world is not in order. This apparent "progress" then provides a spiritual reason for not doing the hard work of maturing.

They are deceived.

I know. I lived that way for almost seventeen years as a Christian. Because of the spiritual growth in certain areas of my life and in those around me, I ignored the reality that signs of emotional immaturity were everywhere in and around me.

Most of us, in our more honest moments, will admit there are deep layers beneath our day-to-day awareness. As the following illustration shows, only about 10 percent of an iceberg is visible to the eye. This 10 percent represents the visible changes we make that others can see. We are nicer people, more respectful. We attend church and participate regularly. We "clean up our lives" somewhat—from alcohol and drugs to foul language to illicit behavior and beyond. We begin to pray and share Christ with others.

Iceberg Model
What Lies Beneath the Surface

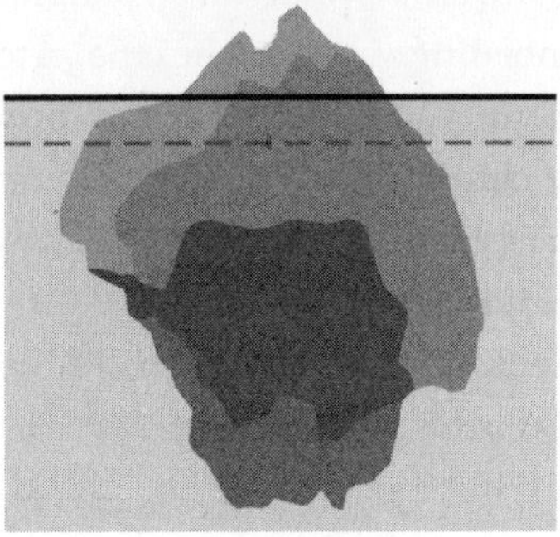

But the roots of who we are continue unaffected and unmoved.

Contemporary spiritual models address some of that 90 percent below the surface. The problem is that a large portion (see the dotted line) remains untouched by Jesus Christ until there is a serious engagement with what I call "emotionally healthy spirituality."

GETTING MY ATTENTION THROUGH PAIN

Three things finally dragged me, kicking and screaming, to open up to the notion of emotionally healthy spirituality.

First, I was not experiencing the joy or contentment Scripture promises us in Christ. I was unhappy, frustrated, overworked, and harried. God had brought me into the Christian life with the offer, "My yoke is easy and my burden is light" (Matthew 11:30), an invitation to a free and abundant life. But I wasn't feeling it.

A yoke, in ancient Palestine, was made of wood, handmade to fit perfectly to the neck and shoulders of oxen and prevent chafing or cutting. In the same way, Jesus' assurance of a "light, easy yoke" can be translated as follows: "I have crafted a life for you, a yoke for you to wear that perfectly fits who you are. It is light and easy, I promise."

The reality, however, is that after many years as an active Christian, I felt exhausted and in need of a break. My life was lived more out of reaction to what other people did or might do or what they thought or might think about me. I knew in my head we were to live to please God. Living like that was another matter. Jesus' yoke felt burdensome.

Second, I was angry, bitter, and depressed. For five years I had attempted to do the work of two or three people. We had two services in English in the morning and one in the afternoon in Spanish. I preached at all of them. When my associate in our afternoon Spanish congregation left the church with two hundred of the two hundred and fifty members to start his own church, I found myself hating him. I tried, without success, to forgive him.

I experienced the growing tension of a double life—preaching love and forgiveness on Sundays and cursing alone in my car on Mondays. The gap between my beliefs and my experience now revealed itself with terrifying clarity.

Third, Geri was lonely, tired of functioning as a single mom with our four daughters. She wanted more from our marriage and grew frustrated enough to finally confront me. She had finally come to a place where she would not accept my excuses, delays, or avoidant behavior. She had nothing else to lose.

Late one evening, as I was sitting on our bed reading, she entered the room and calmly informed me: "Pete, I'd be happier single than married to you. I am getting off this roller coaster. I love you but refuse to live this way anymore. I have waited. . . . I have tried talking to you. You aren't listening. I can't change you. That is up to you. But I am getting on with my life."

She was resolute: "Oh, yes, by the way, the church you pastor? I quit. Your leadership isn't worth following."

For a brief moment, I understood why people murder those they love. She had exposed my nakedness. A part of me wanted to strangle her. Mostly I felt deeply ashamed. It was almost too much for my weak ego to bear.

Nonetheless, this was probably the most loving thing Geri has done for me in our entire marriage. While she could not articulate it yet at that point, she realized something vital: emotional health and spiritual maturity are inseparable. It is not possible to be spiritually mature while remaining emotionally immature.

While I sincerely loved Jesus Christ and believed many truths about him, I was an emotional infant unwilling to look at my immaturity.

Geri's leaving the church pushed me over the brink to look beneath the surface of my iceberg to depths that were, until this time, too frightening to consider. Pain has an amazing ability to open us to new truth and to get us moving. I finally acknowledged the painful truth that huge areas of my life (or iceberg, if you prefer) remained untouched by Jesus Christ. My biblical knowledge, leadership position, seminary training, experience, and skills had not changed that embarrassing reality.

I was engaged in what I now characterize as "emotionally unhealthy spirituality." I was the senior pastor of a church, but I longed to escape and join the ranks of church leavers.

RESPECTING YOUR FULL HUMANITY

God made us as whole people, in his image (see Genesis 1:27). That image includes physical, spiritual, emotional, intellectual, and social dimensions. Take a look at the following illustration:

Different Parts/Components of Who We Are

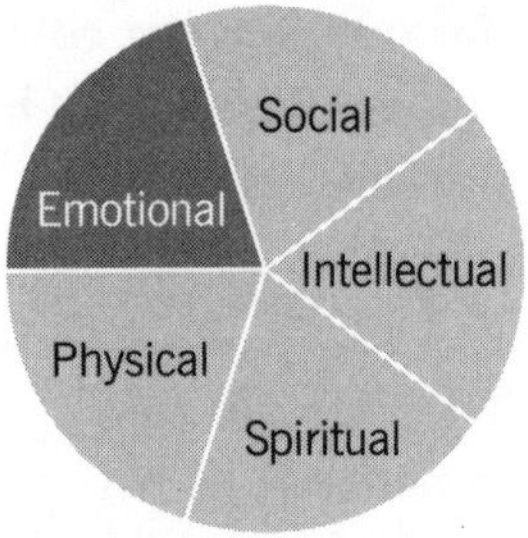

Ignoring any aspect of who we are as men and women made in God's image always results in destructive consequences—in our relationship with God, with others, and with ourselves. If you meet someone, for example, who is mentally challenged or physically disabled, his or her lack of mental or physical development is readily apparent. An autistic child in a crowded playground standing alone for hours without interacting with other children stands out.

Emotional underdevelopment, however, is not so obvious when we first meet people. Over time, as we become involved with them, that reality becomes readily apparent.

I had ignored the "emotional component" in my seeking of God for seventeen years. The spiritual-discipleship approaches of the churches and ministries that had shaped me did not have the language, theology, or training to help me in this area. It didn't matter how many books I read or seminars I attended in the other areas—physical, social, intellectual, spiritual. It didn't matter how many years passed, whether seventeen or another thirty. I would remain an emotional infant until this was exposed and transformed through Jesus Christ. The spiritual foundation upon which I had built my life (and had taught others) was cracked. There was no hiding it from those closest to me.

I had been taught that the way to approach life was through fact, faith, and feelings, in that order. As a result, anger, for example, was simply not important to my walk with God. In fact, it was dangerous and needed to be suppressed. Most people are either "stuffers" or "inflictors" of their anger. Some are both, stuffing it until they finally explode onto others. I was a classic stuffer, asking God to take away my "bad" feelings and make me like Christ.

My failure to "pay attention to God" and to what was going on inside me caused me to miss many gifts. He was lovingly coming and speaking to me, seeking to get me to change. I just wasn't listening. I never expected God to meet me through feelings such as sadness, depression, and anger.

When I finally discovered the link between emotional and spiritual health, a Copernican revolution began for me and there was no going back. This revolutionary link transformed my personal journey with Christ, my marriage, parenting, and, ultimately, New Life Fellowship Church where I pastor.

LIVING GOD'S WAY—A BEAUTIFUL LIFE

Truly, these have been the best twelve years of my life as a human being, husband, father, follower of Jesus, and leader in his church.[2] I learned that if we do the hard work of integrating emotional health and spirituality, we can truly experience the wonderful promises God has given us—for our lives, churches, and communities. God will make our lives beautiful.

The apostle Paul recorded: "What happens when we live [authentically] God's way? He brings gifts into our lives, much the same way that fruit appears in an orchard" (Galatians 5:22 MSG). Using two popular versions of the Bible, let me demonstrate how Paul described these beautiful fruits in Galatians 5:22–23:

NIV	*The Message*
Love	Affection for others
Joy	Exuberance about life
Peace	Serenity
Patience	A willingness to stick with things
Kindness	A sense of compassion in the heart
Goodness	A conviction that a basic holiness permeates things and people
Faithfulness	Involved in loyal commitments
Gentleness	Not needing to force our way in life
Self-Control	Able to marshal and direct our energies wisely

God promises if you and I will do life his way (even though it feels unnatural and hard to us initially), then our lives will be beautiful.

Take a few moments to pause in your reading. Read slowly and prayerfully the previous list, letting each word soak into you. Ask yourself honestly: "To what degree are these fruits realities in my life today?" Think about yourself at home, work, school, church. Allow God to love you where you are now. Ask him to do his work in you, that you might become the kind of person described in the previous passage.

What is so tragic is how few people who desire God, attend and serve their church faithfully, read their Bible, worship, pray, and attend Sunday school classes and small groups do in fact experience the beautiful life, these gifts from God. It goes back, I believe, to a spirituality divorced from emotional health—one that allows deep, underlying layers of our lives to remain untouched by God.

ANOTHER WAY

I believe, however, that the walls we hit in our journey with God are gifts from him. It is not God's intention that we join the ranks of church leavers. He is changing and broadening our understanding of what it means to be a Christ follower in the twenty-first century—in ways far more radical than we ever dreamed. Like with Abraham, he is taking us on a journey with many twists and strange turns in order that deep, experiential life changes might take place in you and me through Jesus Christ.

The sad reality is that most of us will not go forward until the pain of staying where we are is unbearable.

That may be where you are today. Receive your circumstance, then, as his gift to you and open your heart as you read this book to meet him in new and fresh ways.

We can't change—or better said, invite God to change us—when we are unaware and do not see the truth.

In the next chapter we will examine more closely the top ten symptoms of emotionally unhealthy spirituality so we can begin to make the changes God intends.

O God, I thank you for your grace and mercy in my life. If it were not for you, I would not even be aware of you or my need for your transforming work deep beneath the surface of my life. Lord, give me the courage to be honest and to allow the Holy Spirit's power to invade all of who I am below the surface of my iceberg so that Jesus might be formed in me. Lord, help me to grasp how wide and long and high and deep the love of Christ is for me personally. In Jesus' name, amen.

CHAPTER TWO

THE TOP TEN SYMPTOMS OF EMOTIONALLY UNHEALTHY SPIRITUALITY

Diagnosing the Problem

Jay, one of our church members, recently shared with me: "I was a Christian for twenty-two years. But instead of being a twenty-two-year-old Christian, I was a one-year-old Christian twenty-two times! I just kept doing the same things over and over and over again."

Angela, in explaining why she had not attended church for over five years, asked me privately, "Why is it that so many Christians make such lousy human beings?"

Ron, the brother of a member of the small group that meets in our home, upon hearing the title of this book, laughed: "Emotionally healthy spirituality? Isn't that a contradiction?"

Our problem revolves around misapplied biblical truths that not only damage our closest relationships but also obstruct God's work of profoundly transforming us deep beneath the iceberg of our lives.

THE TOP TEN SYMPTOMS OF EMOTIONALLY UNHEALTHY SPIRITUALITY

The pathway for your spiritual life I describe later in this book is radical.

That is, it very likely cuts to the root of your entire approach to following Jesus. Trimming a few branches by, for example, attending a prayer retreat or adding two new spiritual disciplines to an already-crowded life will not be enough. The enormousness of the problem is such that only a revolution in our following of Jesus will bring about the lasting, profound change we long for in our lives.

Before I prescribe this pathway, it is essential for us to clearly identify the primary symptoms of emotionally *unhealthy* spirituality that continue to wreak havoc in our personal lives and our churches. The following are the top ten symptoms indicating if someone is suffering from a bad case of emotionally *unhealthy* spirituality:

1. Using God to run from God
2. Ignoring the emotions of anger, sadness, and fear
3. Dying to the wrong things
4. Denying the past's impact on the present
5. Dividing our lives into "secular" and "sacred" compartments
6. Doing for God instead of being with God
7. Spiritualizing away conflict
8. Covering over brokenness, weakness, and failure
9. Living without limits
10. Judging other people's spiritual journey

1. Using God to Run from God

Few killer viruses are more difficult to discern than this one. On the surface all appears to be healthy and working, but it's not. All those hours and hours spent lost in one Christian book after another . . . all those many Christian responsibilities outside the home or going from one seminar to another . . . all that extra time in prayer and Bible study. . . . At times we use these Christian activities as an unconscious attempt to escape from pain.

In my case, using God to run from God is when I create a great deal of "God-activity" and ignore difficult areas in my life God wants to change. Some examples:

- When I do God's work to satisfy me, not him
- When I do things in his name he never asked me to do
- When my prayers are really about God doing my will, not my surrendering to his
- When I demonstrate "Christian behaviors" so significant people think well of me
- When I focus on certain theological points ("Everything should be done in a fitting and orderly way" [1 Corinthians 14:40]) that are more about my own fears and unresolved issues than concern for God's truth
- When I use his truth to judge and devalue others
- When I exaggerate my accomplishments for God to subtly compete with others
- When I pronounce, "The Lord told me I should do this" when the truth is, "I *think* the Lord told me to do this"
- When I use Scripture to justify the sinful parts of my family, culture, and nation instead of evaluating them under his Lordship
- When I hide behind God talk, deflecting any spotlight on my inner cracks and becoming defensive about my failures
- When I apply biblical truths selectively when it suits my purposes but avoid situations that would require me to make significant life changes

How about an example? John uses God to validate his strong opinions on issues ranging from the appropriate length of women's skirts in church to political candidates to gender roles to his inability to negotiate issues with fellow non-Christian managers at work. He does not listen to or check out the innumerable assumptions he makes about others. He quickly jumps to conclusions. His friends, family, and coworkers find him unsafe and condescending.

John then goes on to convince himself he is doing God's work by misapplying selected verses of Scripture. "Of course that person hates me," he says to himself. "All those who desire to be godly will suffer persecution." Ultimately, however, he is using God to run from God.

2. Ignoring the Emotions of Anger, Sadness, and Fear

Many of us Christians believe wholeheartedly that anger, sadness, and fear are sins to be avoided, indicating something is wrong with our spiritual life. Anger is dangerous and unloving toward others. Sadness indicates a lack of faith in the promises of God; depression surely reveals a life outside the will of God! And fear? The Bible is filled with commands to "not be anxious about anything" and "do not fear" (see Philippians 4:6 and Isaiah 41:10).

So what do we do? We try to inflate ourselves with a false confidence to make those feelings go away. We quote Scripture, pray Scripture, and memorize Scripture—anything to keep ourselves from being overwhelmed by those feelings!

Like most Christians, I was taught that almost all feelings are unreliable and not to be trusted. They go up and down and are the last thing we should be attending to in our spiritual lives. It is true that some Christians live in the extreme of following their feelings in an unhealthy, unbiblical way. It is more common, however, to encounter Christians who do not believe they have permission to admit their feelings or express them openly. This applies especially to the more "difficult" feelings of fear, sadness, shame, anger, hurt, and pain.

Yet how can I listen to what God is saying to me and evaluate what is going on inside of me when I am so imprisoned?

To feel is to be human. To minimize or deny what we feel is a distortion of what it means to be image bearers of our personal God. To the degree that we are unable to express our emotions, we remain impaired in our ability to love God, others, and ourselves well. Yet, as we saw in the previous chapter, our feelings are also a component of what it means to be made in the image of God. To cut them out of our spirituality is to slice off a part of our humanity.

To support what I mistakenly believed about God and my feelings I misapplied the famous illustration below[1]:

Used by permission.

The way I thought my spiritual life should head down the tracks began with the engine, where the driver of the train was *fact*—what God said in Scripture. If I felt angry, for example, I needed to start with fact: "What are you angry about, Pete? So this person lied to you and cheated you. God is on the throne. Jesus was lied to and cheated too. So stop the anger."

After considering the fact of God's truth, I considered my faith—the issue of my will. Did I choose to place my faith in the fact of God's Word? Or did I follow my feelings and "fleshly" inclinations, which were not to be trusted?

At the end of the train was the caboose and what was to be trusted least—my feelings. "Under no circumstances, Pete, rely on your feelings. The heart is sinful and desperately wicked. Who can understand it [see Jeremiah 17:9]? This will only lead you astray into sin."

When taken in its entirety the practical implications of such an imbalanced, narrow, biblical belief system are, as we shall see later, enormous. It leads to a devaluing and repression of the emotional aspect of our humanity that is also made in the image of God. Sadly, some of our Christian beliefs and expectations today have, as Thomas Merton wrote, "merely deadened our humanity, instead of setting it free to develop richly, in all its capacities, under the influence of grace."[2]

3. Dying to the Wrong Things

As Iraneus said many centuries ago, "The glory of God is a human being fully alive."

True, Jesus did say, "If anyone would come after me, he must deny himself and take up his cross daily and follow me" (Luke 9:23). But when we apply this verse rigidly, without qualification from the rest of Scripture, it leads to the very opposite of what God intends. It results in a narrow, faulty theology that says, "The more miserable you are, the more you suffer, the more God loves you. Disregard your unique personhood; it has no place in God's kingdom."

We are to die to the sinful parts of who we are—such as defensiveness, detachment from others, arrogance, stubbornness, hypocrisy, judgmentalism, a lack of vulnerability—as well as the more obvious sins described for us in Scripture: Do not murder. Do not steal. Do not bear false witness. Speak the truth (see Exodus 20:13–16 and Ephesians 4:25).

We are not called by God to die to the "good" parts of who we are. God never asked us to die to the healthy desires and pleasures of life—to friendships, joy, art, music, beauty, recreation, laughter, and nature. God plants desires in our hearts so we will nurture and water them. Often these desires and passions are invitations from God, gifts from him. Yet somehow we feel guilty unwrapping those presents.

When I ask people, "Tell me about your wishes, hopes, and dreams," they are often speechless.

"Why do you ask?" they respond. "Isn't my only wish, hope, and dream supposed to be to serve Jesus?"

Not exactly. God never asks us to annihilate the self. We are not to become "non-persons" when we become Christians. The very opposite is true. God intends our deeper, truer self, which he created, to blossom freely as we follow him. God has endowed each of us with certain essential qualities that reflect and express him in a unique way. Part of the sanctification process of the Holy Spirit is to strip away the false constructs we have accumulated and enable our true selves to emerge.

4. Denying the Past's Impact on the Present

When we come to faith in Jesus Christ, whether as a child, teenager, or adult, we are, in the dramatic language of the Bible, born again (see John 3:3). The apostle Paul describes it this way: "The old has gone, the new has come!" (2 Corinthians 5:17).

These two verses and their meanings, however, are sometimes misunderstood. Yes, it is true that when we come to Christ, our sins are wiped away and we are given a new name, a new identity, a new future, a new life. It is truly a miracle. We are declared righteous before God through the life, death, and resurrection of Jesus (see Philippians 3:9–10). The eternal, holy God of the universe is no longer our judge but our Father. That is the great news of the gospel.

But we need to understand this does not mean that what our past lives were won't continue to influence us in different ways. I was under the illusion for years that because I accepted Jesus, my old life was no longer in me. My past before Christ was painful. I wanted to forget it. I never wanted to look back. Life was so much better now that Jesus was with me.

I thought I was free.

Geri, after nine years of marriage, knew better. I will never forget the first time we made a genogram—a diagram outlining some of the patterns of our families. Our counselor at the time took about an hour to ask probing questions about the interactions between members of both of our families, to write two or three adjectives to describe our parents and their relationships.

When the counselor finished, he simply asked us, "Do you see any similarities between your marriage and your parents'?"

We both sat there dumbfounded.

We were evangelical Christians. We were committed and stable. Our priorities and life choices were very different from that of our parents. Yet, underneath the surface, our marriage bore a striking resemblance to that of our parents'. Gender roles; the handling of anger and conflict and shame; how we defined success; our view of family, children, recreation, pleasure, sexuality, grieving; and our relationships with friends had all been shaped by our families of origin and our cultures.

Sitting in that counselor's office that day, embarrassed by the state of our marriage, we learned a lesson we would never forget: even though we had been committed Christians for almost twenty years, our ways of relating mirrored much more our family of origin than the way God intended for his new family in Christ.

The work of growing in Christ (what theologians call *sanctification*) does not mean we don't go back to the past as we press ahead to what God has for us. It actually demands we go back in order to break free from unhealthy and destructive patterns that prevent us from loving ourselves and others as God designed.

5. Dividing Our Lives into "Secular" and "Sacred" Compartments

Human beings have an uncanny ability to live compartmentalized, double lives.

Frank attends church and sings about God's love. On the way home he pronounces the death penalty over another driver. For Frank Sunday church is for God. Monday to Saturday is for work.

Jane yells at her husband, berating him for his lack of spiritual leadership with the children. He walks away deflated and crushed. She walks away convinced she has fought valiantly in God's name.

Ken has a disciplined devotional time with God each day before going to work, but then does not think of God's presence with him all through the day at work or when he returns home to be with his wife and children.

Judith cries during songs about the love and grace of God at her church. But she regularly complains and blames others for the difficulties and trials in her life.

It is so easy to compartmentalize God to "Christian activities" around church and our spiritual disciplines without thinking of him in our marriages, the disciplining of our children, the spending of our money, our recreation, or even our studying for exams. According to Gallup polls and sociologists, one of the greatest scandals of our day is that "evangelical Christians are as likely to embrace lifestyles every bit as hedonistic, materialistic, self-centered and sexually immoral as the world in general."[3] The statistics are devastating:

- Church members divorce their spouses as often as their secular neighbors.
- Church members beat their wives as often as their neighbors.
- Church members' giving patterns indicate they are almost as materialistic as non-Christians.
- White evangelicals are the most likely people to object to neighbors of another race.
- Of the "higher-commitment" evangelicals, 26 percent think premarital sex is acceptable, while 46 percent of "lower-commitment" evangelicals believe it to be okay also.[4]

Ron Sider, in his book *The Scandal of the Evangelical Conscience*, summarizes the level of our compartmentalization: "Whether the issue is marriage and sexuality or money and care for the poor, evangelicals today are living scandalously unbiblical lives. . . . The data suggest that in many crucial areas evangelicals are not living any differently from their unbelieving neighbors."[5]

The consequences of this on our witness to Jesus Christ are incalculable, both for ourselves and the world around us. We miss out on the genuine joy of life with Jesus Christ that he promises (see John 15:11). And the watching world shakes its head, incredulous that we can be so blind we can't see the large gap between our words and our everyday lives.

6. Doing for God Instead of Being with God

Being productive and getting things done are high priorities in our Western culture. Praying and enjoying God's presence for no other reason than to delight in him was a luxury, I was told, that we could take pleasure in once we got to heaven. For now, there was too much to be done. People were lost. The world was in deep trouble. And God had entrusted us with the good news of the gospel.

For most of my Christian life I wondered if monks were truly Christian. Their lifestyle seemed escapist. Surely they were not in the will of God. What were they doing to spread the gospel in a world dying without Christ? What about all the sheep who were lost and without direction? Didn't they know the laborers are few (see Matthew 9:37)?

The messages were clear:

- Doing lots of work for God is a sure sign of a growing spirituality.
- It is all up to you. And you'll never finish while you're alive on earth.
- God can't move unless you pray.
- You are responsible to share Christ around you at all times or people will go to hell.
- Things will fall apart if you don't persevere and hold things together.

Are all these things wrong? No. But work *for* God that is not nourished by a deep interior life *with* God will eventually be contaminated by other things such as ego, power, needing approval of and from others, and buying into the wrong ideas of success and the mistaken belief that we can't fail. When we work for God because of these things, our experience of the gospel often falls off center. We become "human doings" not "human beings." Our experiential sense of worth and validation gradually shifts from God's unconditional love for us in Christ to our works and performance. The joy of Christ gradually disappears.

Our activity for God can only properly flow from a life *with* God. We cannot give what we do not possess. Doing for God in a way that is proportionate to our being with God is the only pathway to a pure heart and seeing God (see Matthew 5:8).

7. Spiritualizing Away Conflict

Nobody likes conflict. Yet conflict is everywhere—from law courts to workplaces to classrooms to neighborhoods to marriages to parenting our children to close friendships to when someone has spoken or acted toward you inappropriately. But the belief that smoothing over disagreements or "sweeping them under the rug" is to follow Jesus continues to be one of the most destructive myths alive in the church today. For this reason, churches, small groups, ministry teams, denominations, and communities continue to experience the pain of unresolved conflicts.

Very, very few of us come from families where conflicts are resolved in a mature, healthy way. Most simply bury our tensions and move on. In my own family, when I became a Christian I was the great "peacemaker." I would do anything to keep unity and love flowing in the church as well as my marriage and family. I saw conflict as something that had to be fixed as quickly as possible. Like radioactive waste from a nuclear power plant, if not contained, I feared it might unleash terrible damage.

So I did what most Christians do: I lied a lot, both to myself and others.

What do you do when faced with the tension and mess of disagreements? Some of us may be guilty of one or more of the following:

- Say one thing to people's faces and then another behind their backs
- Make promises we have no intention of keeping
- Blame
- Attack
- Give people the silent treatment
- Become sarcastic
- Give in because we are afraid of not being liked
- "Leak" our anger by sending an e-mail containing a not-so-subtle criticism
- Tell only half the truth because we can't bear to hurt a friend's feelings
- Say yes when we mean no
- Avoid and withdraw and cut off
- Find an outside person with whom we can share in order to ease our anxiety

Jesus shows us that healthy Christians do not avoid conflict. His life was filled with it! He was in regular conflict with the religious leaders, the crowds, the disciples—even his own family. Out of a desire to bring true peace, Jesus disrupted the false peace all around him. He refused to "spiritualize away" conflict.

8. Covering Over Brokenness, Weakness, and Failure

The pressure to present an image of ourselves as strong and spiritually "together" hovers over most of us. We feel guilty for not measuring up, for not making the grade. We forget that not one of us is perfect and that we are all sinners. We forget that David, one of God's most beloved friends, committed adultery with Bathsheba and murdered her husband. Talk about a scandal! How many of us would not have erased that from the history books forever lest the name of God be disgraced?

David did not. Instead he used his absolute power as king to ensure the details of his colossal failure were published in the history books for all future generations! In fact, David wrote a song about his failure to be sung in Israel's worship services and to be published in their worship manual, the psalms. (Hopefully he asked Bathsheba's permission first!) David knew "the sacrifices of God are a broken spirit; a broken and contrite heart, O God, you will not despise" (Psalm 51:17).

Another of God's great men, the apostle Paul, wrote about God not answering his prayers and about his "thorn in [the] flesh." He thanked God for his brokenness, reminding his readers that Christ's power "is made perfect in weakness" (2 Corinthians 12:7–10). How many Christians do you know who would do such a thing today?

The Bible does not spin the flaws and weaknesses of its heroes. Moses was a murderer. Hosea's wife was a prostitute. Peter rebuked God! Noah got drunk. Jonah was a racist. Jacob was a liar. John Mark deserted Paul. Elijah burned out. Jeremiah was depressed and suicidal. Thomas doubted. Moses had a temper. Timothy had ulcers. And all these people send the same message: that every human being on earth, regardless of their gifts and strengths, is weak, vulnerable, and dependent on God and others.

For years I would observe unusually gifted people perform in extraordinary ways—whether in the arts, sports, leadership, politics, business, academics, parenting, or church—and wonder if somehow they were not as broken as the rest of us. Now I know they weren't. We are all deeply flawed and broken. There are no exceptions.

9. Living Without Limits

I was taught that good Christians constantly give and tend to others. I wasn't supposed to say no to opportunities to or requests for help because that would be selfish.

Some Christians are selfish. They believe in God and Jesus Christ, but live their lives as if God doesn't exist. They don't think or care about loving and serving others outside of their families and friends. That is a tragedy.

I meet many more Christians, however, who carry around guilt for never doing enough. "Pete, I spent two hours on the phone listening to him and it still wasn't enough," a friend recently complained to me. "It makes me want to run away."

This guilt often leads to discouragement. And this discouragement often leads Christians to disengagement and isolation from "needy people" because they don't know what else to do.

The core spiritual issue here relates to our limits and our humanity. We are not God. We cannot serve everyone in need. We are human. When Paul said, "I can do everything through him who gives me strength" (Philippians 4:13), the context was that of learning to be content in all circumstances. The strength he received from Christ was not the strength to change, deny, or defy his circumstances; it was the strength to be content in the midst of them, to surrender to God's loving will for him (see Philippians 4:11–13).

Jesus modeled this for us as a human being—fully God yet fully human. He did not heal every sick person in Palestine. He did not raise every dead person. He did not feed all the hungry beggars or set up job development centers for the poor of Jerusalem.

He didn't do it, and we shouldn't feel we have to. But somehow we do. Why don't we take appropriate care of ourselves? Why are so many Christians, along with the rest of our culture, frantic, exhausted, overloaded, and hurried?

Few Christians make the connection between love of self and love of others. Sadly, many believe that taking care of themselves is a sin, a "psychologizing" of the gospel taken from our self-centered culture. I believed that myself for years.

It is true we are called to consider others more important than ourselves (see Philippians 2:3). We are called to lay down our lives for others (see 1 John 3:16). But remember, you first need a "self" to lay down.

As Parker Palmer said, "Self-care is never a selfish act—it is simply good stewardship of the only gift I have, the gift I was put on earth to offer others. Anytime we can listen to true self and give it the care it requires, we do it not only for ourselves, but for the many others whose lives we touch."[6]

10. Judging Other People's Spiritual Journey

"The monk," said one of the Desert Fathers, "must die to his neighbor and never judge him at all in any way whatever." He continued: "If you are occupied with your own faults, you have no time to see those of your neighbor."[7]

I was taught it was my responsibility to correct people in error or in sin and to always counsel people who were mixed up spiritually. I therefore felt guilty if I saw something questionable and did nothing to point it out. But I felt even guiltier when I was supposed to fix someone's problem and had to admit "I don't know how" or "I don't know what to say." Wasn't I commanded to be ready to give an answer for the hope that is in me (see 1 Peter 3:15)?

Of course, many of us have no trouble at all dispensing advice or pointing out wrongdoing. We spend so much time at it that we end up self-deceived, thinking we have much to give and therefore little to receive from others. After all, we're the ones who are right, aren't we? This often leads to an inability to receive from ordinary, less mature people than ourselves. We only receive from experts or professionals.

This has always been one of the greatest dangers in Christianity. It becomes "us versus them." In Jesus' day there was the superior "in group" of Pharisees who obeyed God's commands. And there was the inferior "out group" of sinners, tax collectors, and prostitutes.

Sadly, we often turn our differences into moral superiority or virtues. I see it all the time. We judge people for their music (too soft or too loud) and the length of their hair (too short or too long). We judge them for dressing up or dressing down, for the movies they watch and the cars they buy. We create never-ending groups to subtly categorize people:

- "Those artists and musicians. They are so flakey."
- "Those engineers. They are so cerebral. They're cold as fish."
- "Men are idiots. They're socially infantile."
- "Women are overly sensitive and emotional."
- "The rich are self-indulgent and selfish."
- "The poor are lazy."

We judge the Presbyterians for being too structured. We judge the Pentecostals for lacking structure. We judge Episcopalians for their candles and their written prayers. We judge Roman Catholics for their view of the Lord's Supper and Orthodox Christians from the Eastern part of the world for their strange culture and love for icons.

By failing to let others be themselves before God and move at their own pace, we inevitably project onto them our own discomfort with their choice to live life differently than we do. We end up eliminating them in our minds, trying to make others like us, abandoning them altogether or falling into a "Who cares?" indifference toward them. In some ways the silence of unconcern can be more deadly than hate.

Like Jesus said, unless I first take the log out of my own eye, knowing that I have huge blind spots, I am dangerous. I must see the extensive damage sin has done to every part of who I am—emotion, intellect, body, will, and spirit—before I can attempt to remove the speck from my brother's eye (see Matthew 7:1–5).

THE REVOLUTIONARY ANTIDOTE

The pathway to unleashing the transformative power of Jesus to heal our spiritual lives can be found in the joining of emotional health and contemplative spirituality. In the next chapter I will explain what they are and why they both must be integrated into our discipleship with Christ.

Lord, when I consider this chapter, the only thing I can say is, "Lord Jesus Christ, have mercy on me, a sinner." Thank you, O God, that I stand before you in the righteousness of Jesus, in his perfect record and performance, not my own. Lord, I ask that you would not simply heal the symptoms of what is not right in my life, but that you would surgically remove all that is in me that does not belong to you. As I think about what I have read, Lord, pour light over the things that are hidden. May I see clearly as you hold me tenderly. In Jesus' name, amen.

CHAPTER THREE

THE RADICAL ANTIDOTE: EMOTIONAL HEALTH AND CONTEMPLATIVE SPIRITUALITY

Bringing Transformation to the Deep Places

Many Christians are stuck. Some are lost this very moment, trying to find their way. Others are afraid they will go astray if they remain stuck for too much longer. More than a few are lost without knowing it.

GETTING STUCK

Once people begin their journey with Jesus Christ and join a church or community, our first task is to help them connect with God and grow spiritually. Our sincere hope is that they will allow the Word and the Spirit to transform each aspect of their lives. We teach them to:

- attend church each week for worship, the Word, and, in some traditions, to participate in the Lord's Supper;
- have a quiet time (some call it *devotions*), preferably at the start of each day;
- participate in a small group or Sunday school class for spiritual nourishment, fellowship, and the study of Scripture;

- trust God by giving financially to God's work;
- let Christ inform the way they behave at work, home, school, and in all other relationships;
- discover and use their spiritual gift inside the church and serve somewhere—as an usher, greeter, small-group leader, or board member;
- evangelize by telling others who do not know Jesus how they were "blind but now see" and inviting them to church events as appropriate; and
- attend retreats and conferences, read books, and listen to tapes to continue growing.

All the previous are excellent steps to begin a journey with Christ. Yet they are simply not enough. After a few years many find that past, deeply rooted behavioral patterns that move them away from Christ remain entrenched. And what we're teaching them simply isn't enough to combat those patterns. What most people are left with is a long list of things to do and not to do—ten new things to feel guilty about messing up on.

What is needed is the injection of an antidote into all aspects of the Christian life—an antidote that turns our spiritual lives right side up. I'm talking about *emotional health* and *contemplative spirituality*. Together these two unleash a revolution in our lives, positioning us so that God can mold us into the men and women he has called us to be.

Before I explain what this radical remedy is and why it is required, however, we need to step back and appreciate why it is so difficult to follow Jesus today. What are the hurricane winds, internal and external, that prevent us from becoming all God intends? In order to gain insight, I turn momentarily to the book of Revelation where we are given a picture of the very real gale winds that oppose us and keep us from deep transformation.

REVELATION AND THE BEAST

The reason Revelation is such an important book for us today is it teaches us about our life-and-death struggle to remain truly connected to God and the choices before us.

Revelation, one of the most badly interpreted and misunderstood books of the Bible, contains the key to why most present-day Christians are overwhelmed by the culture and the world around us: we underestimate the intensity and power of evil—both outside and inside of us.

The Beast Yesterday

The book of Revelation was written to Christians suffering terrible persecution living in the province of Asia (present-day Turkey) between A.D. 90 and 95. To get his message across, the apostle John used pictures and images familiar to his readers to enable them to see clearly what was *really* going on around them.

As the New Testament scholar Richard Bauckham noted, the book of Revelation pictures the Roman Empire as "the beast." The Roman culture, economy, education, and military might brought great wealth and peace to their empire. People were excited about Roman rule. Rome proclaimed herself the eternal city, offering security and the possibilities of dazzling wealth. The whole world envied her prosperity and affluence.[1] The apostle John wrote: "The whole world was astonished and followed the beast. . . . They also worshiped the beast and asked, 'Who is like the beast? Who can make war against him?'" (Revelation 13:3–4).

As a result, the faith of many Christians was tested. Rome demanded their allegiance. If they did not submit to the pressure, they lost jobs, privileges, reputations, hard-earned prosperity, and friends. Some quit their faith altogether, finding the pressure of going against the intense, seemingly irresistible, pressure of Rome too much to bear. Still other believers were trying to find a middle ground between the values of the Roman culture (the beast) and the values of Christ. They tried to simultaneously keep one foot in the world of the beast and one foot in the world of Christ. They simply assimilated into the culture around them.

God, through Revelation, makes clear that no compromise is possible between Christ and the beast. We have only two choices: either we compromise and allow ourselves to be absorbed into the culture of the beast, or we "come out of her" (Revelation 18:4), faithfully bearing witness to what is true by both our words and our lives.

The book of Revelation also wants us to understand that *behind* the beast is a ferocious dragon with tremendous size and awesome power. This dragon, in Revelation, represents active, powerful, satanic power. In other words, Satan was using the Roman Empire to cut believers off, by any means possible, from a living relationship with Jesus:

"The great dragon was hurled down—that ancient serpent called the devil, or Satan, who leads the whole world astray. . . . Then the dragon was enraged . . . and went off to make war against the rest of her offspring—those who obey God's commandments and hold to the testimony of Jesus" (Revelation 12:9, 17).

The Beast Today

The message of Revelation is that in all history, in all parts of the world, believers must resist and overcome the beast expressed through the culture of their generation: "This calls for patient endurance and faithfulness on the part of the saints" (Revelation 13:10). Therefore, it is essential we see clearly how the beast threatens the church and absorbs Christians in our day. As Os Guiness wrote, due to the combination of capitalism, technology, and modern communications, the most powerful civilization ever—a global culture—has been formed.[2] This global culture is the beast that threatens to swallow us in these days. The core values of the beast in the twenty-first century scream at us from computers, billboards, televisions, DVDs, music, schools, newspapers, magazines, and iPods. The beast tells us:

- happiness is found in having things;
- you should get all you can for yourself, as quickly as you can;
- security is found in money, power, status, and good health;
- above all, you should seek all the pleasure, convenience, and comfort you can;
- God is irrelevant to everyday life;
- Christianity is just one of many alternative spiritualities;
- there are no moral absolutes; whatever is true for you is what is true;

- you're not responsible for anyone but yourself; and
- this life on earth is all there is.

Like goldfish swimming in the middle of the Pacific Ocean unaware they are in water, we, too, live oblivious to our beast. Like the Christians in the first century, we live in a culture shaped by the beast. We eat, drink, drive, watch television and movies, attend schools, shop, work, raise families, listen to the music, and even participate in churches within a society shaped by the beast. This feeds the fire of the "beast" within us. I am referring to the fears, the mistrust, the fierce self-will, the stubbornness, and the rebellion in our very depths.

The apostle Paul had the courage to look at his own inner wretchedness. He observed this about himself: "So I find this law at work: When I want to do good, evil is right there with me. For in my inner being I delight in God's law; but I see another law at work in the members of my body, waging war against the law of my mind and making me a prisoner of the law of sin at work within my members. What a wretched man I am! Who will rescue me from this body of death?" (Romans 7:21–24).

Paul saw his own untamable monsters within, the chaotic blur of energies, the seemingly uncontrollable forces of his sinful nature.

What do we see inside ourselves? Many of us are afraid to even look. Our most natural prayer is "*My* Father in heaven, hallowed be *my* name, may *my* kingdom come, may *my* will be done on earth." We're afraid of God's will being done because we can't control what he will do, when he will do it, how he will do it, and what the outcome might be. God's will requires surrender and trust, and it's something we're unwilling to offer.

Is it any wonder, then, that our primary question is: "What can Jesus do for me? Can he make me more prosperous, well-adjusted, and peaceful?" The beast has so taken captive the church that many of us act as if God works for us, functioning as our personal assistant when we need him. We, in effect, use God, squeezing him into our image of what he should be like. When he allows suffering in our lives, we get mad at him and pout. How dare he?

Yes, the sin of our first parents marks and stains all of us. Our minds and wills resist the light and prefer the darkness. The more we thrash around in the soup of sin, the deeper we sink. The only way out is a salvation that comes from a power that stands outside of the mess in which we find ourselves. Only God intervening in the person of Jesus to live and die on the cross on our behalf could rescue us from our helpless condition in sin.

Jesus is the Savior of the world. Only an "alien righteousness," as Martin Luther called it,[3] offering us a perfect record that is not our own, can save us. For this reason the gospel truly is the greatest news on the face of the earth.

UNLEASHING A REVOLUTION

Salvation is a gift of grace. But is it any wonder, in light of the reality of the beast outside us, and our sinfulness within, why so few people experience deep, ongoing transformation in their following of Christ?

A person can grow emotionally healthy without Christ. In fact, I can think of a number of non-Christian people who are more loving, balanced, and civil than many church members I know (including myself!). At the same time, a person can be deeply committed to contemplative spirituality, even to the point of taking a monastic vow, and remain emotionally unaware and socially maladjusted.

How can this be?

Few Christians committed to contemplative spirituality integrate the inner workings of emotional health. At the same time few people committed to emotional health integrate contemplative spirituality. Both are powerful, life-changing emphases when engaged in separately. But *together* they offer nothing short of a spiritual revolution, transforming the hidden places deep beneath the surface. When emotional health and contemplative spirituality are interwoven together in an individual's life, a small group, a church, a university fellowship, or a community, people's lives are dramatically transformed. They work as an antidote to heal the symptoms of emotionally unhealthy spirituality described in chapter two. Moreover, they provide a means to decisively conquer the beast within us and in our culture.

DEFINING EMOTIONAL HEALTH AND CONTEMPLATIVE SPIRITUALITY

Emotional health is concerned with such things as:[4]

- naming, recognizing, and managing our own feelings;
- identifying with and having active compassion for others;
- initiating and maintaining close and meaningful relationships;
- breaking free from self-destructive patterns;
- being aware of how our past impacts our present;
- developing the capacity to express our thoughts and feelings clearly, both verbally and nonverbally;
- respecting and loving others without having to change them;
- asking for what we need, want, or prefer clearly, directly, and respectfully;
- accurately self-assessing our strengths, limits, and weaknesses and freely sharing them with others;
- learning the capacity to resolve conflict maturely and negotiate solutions that consider the perspectives of others;
- distinguishing and appropriately expressing our sexuality and sensuality; and
- grieving well.

Contemplative spirituality, on the other hand, focuses on classic practices and concerns such as:[5]

- awakening and surrendering to God's love in any and every situation;
- positioning ourselves to hear God and remember his presence in all we do;
- communing with God, allowing him to fully indwell the depth of our being;
- practicing silence, solitude, and a life of unceasing prayer;
- resting attentively in the presence of God;
- understanding our earthly life as a journey of transformation toward ever-increasing union with God;

- finding the true essence of who we are in God;
- loving others out of a life of love for God;
- developing a balanced, harmonious rhythm of life that enables us to be aware of the sacred in all of life;
- adapting historic practices of spirituality that are applicable today;
- allowing our Christian lives to be shaped by the rhythms of the Christian calendar rather than the culture; and
- living in committed community that passionately loves Jesus above all else.

The combination of emotional health and contemplative spirituality addresses what I believe to be the missing piece in contemporary Christianity. Together they unleash the Holy Spirit inside us in order that we might know experientially the power of an authentic life in Christ.

JOINING THE TWO TOGETHER

The following[6] illustrates well how contemplation and emotional health are different and yet overlap. In a very real sense, both are necessary to loving God, loving ourselves, and loving others. For this reason, these form the outer circle around the diagram.

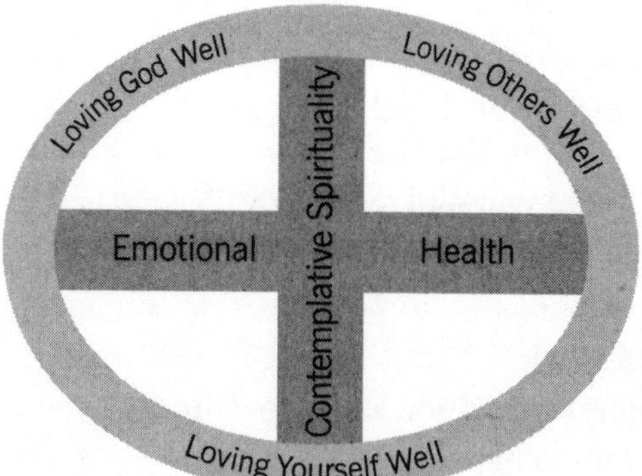

The greatest commandments, Jesus said, are that we love God with all our heart, mind, strength, and soul and that we love our neighbor as ourselves (see Matthew 22:37–40). Contemplation has been defined in many ways through history. Brother Lawrence called it "the pure loving gaze that finds God everywhere." Francis de Sale describes it as "the mind's loving, unmixed, permanent attention to the things of God." For this reason, contemplation is the vertical line going upward toward God that cuts through emotional health. We are not simply about experiencing a better quality of life through emotional health. Awareness of and responding to the love of God is at the heart of our lives. We are first and foremost about God revealed in Christ.

At the same time contemplation is not simply about our relationship with God. It is ultimately the way we see and treat people and the way we look at ourselves. Our relationship with God and relationship with others are two sides of the same coin. If our contemplation or "loving union with God" does not result in a loving union with people, then it is, as 1 John 4:7–21 says so eloquently, not true. Moreover, as we shall see, it is about seeing God in all of life.

Emotional health, on the other hand, concerns itself primarily with loving others well. It connects us to our interiors, making possible the seeing and treating of each individual as worthy of respect, created in the image of God and not just as objects to use. For this reason, self-awareness, knowing what is going on inside of us, is indispensable to emotional health and loving well. In fact, the extent to which we love and respect ourselves is the extent to which we will be able to love and respect others.

At the same time, emotional health is not only about ourselves and our relationships; it impacts our image of God, our hearing of God's voice, and our discernment of his will.

THE THREE GIFTS OF INTEGRATION

Emotional health and contemplative spirituality offer three primary gifts. Each enables us to participate in the enormous transformative power of Jesus Christ today. They are:

- the gift of slowing down;
- the gift of anchoring in God's love; and
- the gift of breaking free from illusions.

1. The Gift of Slowing Down

Almost everyone is busy. Whether a teenager or a senior citizen, a mom at home with small children or a corporate executive, a teacher or a student, rich or poor, Christian or not, we are overscheduled, tense, frantic, preoccupied, fatigued, and starved for time. Others are not busy but bored, ignoring God's presence and gifts all around us.

Of course, we were bred to be that way. Activism is the key explanation for how evangelicals came to dominate the English-speaking world from 1850 to 1900. Working hard for God, "in season and out of season," was expected for church members. Charles Spurgeon, one of the greatest evangelical figures of church history, summed up our commitment to activism in a speech he gave to future leaders training for the ministry: "Brethren, do something; do something; do something. While committees waste their time over resolutions, do something."[7]

Our greatest weakness flows out of our greatest strength. We excel at leading people to a personal relationship with Jesus and mobilizing the church to go out and make disciples of all nations. But because of that excellence we often do not pay attention to God. We are too active for the kind of reflection needed to sustain a life of love with God and others.

Emotional health and contemplative spirituality together are powerful enough to slow us down. But the issue is not simply slowing down. You may be slowing down, but the real question is, are you paying attention to God? Emotional health and contemplative spirituality call us to *reflection* so that we might listen to God and to ourselves. Let's take a look at how each side works.

CONTEMPLATIVE SPIRITUALITY

> As Jesus and his disciples were on their way, he came to a village where a woman named Martha opened her home to him. She had a sister called Mary, who sat at the Lord's feet listening to what he said. But Martha was distracted by all the preparations that had to be made. She came to him and asked, "Lord, don't you care that my sister has left me to do the work by myself? Tell her to help me!" "Martha, Martha," the Lord answered, "you are worried and upset about many things, but

> only one thing is needed. Mary has chosen what is better, and it will not be taken away from her." (Luke 10:38–42)

Mary and Martha represent two approaches to the Christian life. Martha is actively serving Jesus, but she is missing Jesus. She is busy in the "doing" of life. Her life, at this moment, is filled with "shoulds" and "have tos." Her life is fragmented, pressured, and filled with distractions. Her duties have become disconnected from her love for Jesus.

Martha's problem goes beyond her busyness. Her life is uncentered and divided. I suspect that if Martha were to sit at the feet of Jesus, she would still be distracted with everything on her mind. Her inner person is touchy, irritable, and anxious. One of the surest signs of her life being out of order is that she even tells God what to do!

Mary, on the other hand, is sitting at the feet of Jesus, listening to him. She is "being" with Jesus, enjoying intimacy with him, loving him, attentive, open, quiet, taking pleasure in his presence. She is engaged in what we will call the contemplative life.

Mary is not trying to master God. Her life has one center of gravity —Jesus. I suspect that if Mary were to help with the many household chores, she would not be worried or upset. Why? Her inner person has slowed down enough to focus on Jesus and to center her life on him.

When I became a Christian I fell in love with Jesus. I cherished time alone with him reading the Bible and praying. Yet almost immediately, the activity circle of my life (i.e., the "doing") fell out of balance with the contemplative circle (i.e., "being" with Jesus). Like everyone around me, I, too, struggled with a desire for more time with God, but there was simply too much to do. See the following illustration:

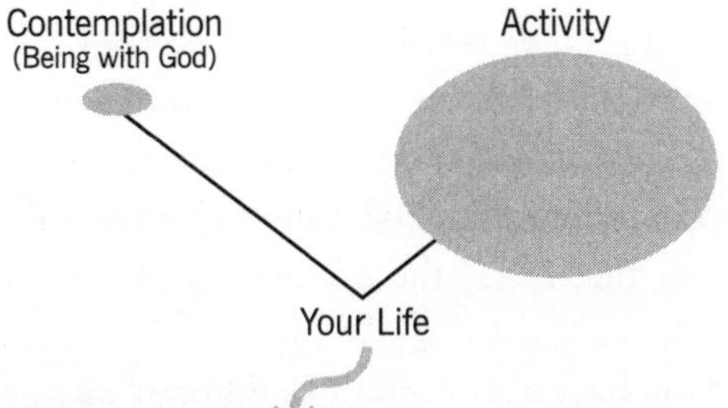

The twisted arrow below "Your Life" illustrates the result of the imbalance in my contemplation and activity. I often felt off center. Church leaders taught me early on about the importance of quiet time or devotions to nurture my personal relationship with Christ. It simply was not enough. The message of activism within my evangelical tradition drowned out any emphasis on contemplation.

In every generation, Christians have written on the balance of Mary and Martha in our lives. They all sound the same theme: the active life in the world *for* God can only properly flow from a life *with* God. God has a unique combination of activity and contemplation for each of us. See this new illustration:

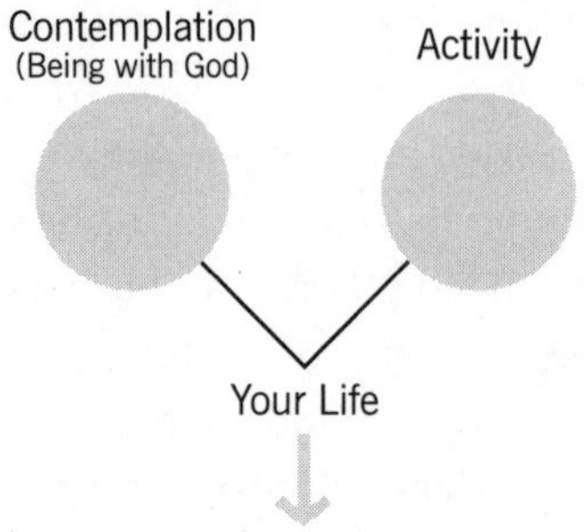

When we gain the ability to integrate activity with contemplation, we find the arrow of our lives has a beauty, a harmony, and a clarity that makes "doing" life straightforward and joyful.

The reason we need to stop and be with God is so we might create a continual and easy familiarity with God's presence at all times—while working, playing, cooking, taking out the garbage, driving, visiting friends, as well as during worship, prayer, and Bible study. This requires that we slow down to pay attention. Our goal is to love God with our whole being, to be consistently conscious of God through our daily life—whether it is when we are stopped like Mary, sitting at the feet of Jesus, or active like Martha, taking care of the tasks of life. We know we have found our balance when we are so deeply rooted in God that our activity is marked by the peaceful, joyful, rich quality of our contemplation.

Of course, God has made each of us different. The question is how much time we need to be alone with God so that Christ's life flows out of ours. Your combination of activity and contemplation will be different from mine. God has crafted each of our personalities, temperaments, life situations, passions, and callings in a unique way.

Another way to discover how much we need to slow down relates to how attentive we are to God during our activity. God speaks to each one of us every day—through Scripture, creation, dreams, silence, traffic jams, boring workdays, interruptions, conflicts, job losses, relationship breakdowns, successes, failures, and betrayals. Jesus described this as his "sowing of seeds." Our problem is that many of these seeds are "snatched away immediately" or die prematurely due to external pressures or our absorption with other interests and concerns (see Mark 4:1–20). Most of these seeds are lost because we do not pay attention.[8]

When I have sufficient "slowing-down time" alone, I find that my activity is marked by a deep, loving communion with God. Then Christ's life, more often than not, flows through me to others.

You may actually be wondering how to slow down to pay attention to God continually. Stay with me. The answer will slowly unfold in the chapters to follow. For now let's continue with our current topic.

EMOTIONAL HEALTH

The pace of my life slowed down considerably eleven years ago when I began my journey into emotional health. It takes time—lots of it—to feel, to grieve, to listen, to reflect, to be mindful of what is going on around us and in us, to live and not simply exist, and to love well. Resolving to reflect and grow in emotional health helped me to understand 1 Corinthians 13 for the first time: the goal of the Christian life is to love well. The apostle Paul says that we can do great miracles, have great faith, and sacrifice everything we have and yet remain spiritually a baby—or perhaps not even be a Christian at all. Genuine fruit, he argues, is marked by supernatural love working in and through us (see 1 Corinthians 13:1–13).

Understanding this required a radical shift in my priorities. Three things came to the forefront:

HOME: I had to carve out time to love Geri and each of our four daughters. Loving Jesus through investing in our marriage and in parenting slowed me down considerably. For example, I stopped sneaking work in during my daughters' soccer games or when we were playing a board game together. My expectations and goals for work diminished. My expectations and goals for time to cultivate friendship with Geri and our four girls soared. There is no way to get around the serious time investment needed for a high-quality marriage and family.

WORK: I also needed to find time to listen to and be present to the staff who worked for me, as well as others around me. To do this I had to stop planning too many appointments and meetings in too little time. Our decision making and discernment as a staff also began to change. We slowed down enough (at least more than before!) to pause and be quiet enough to recognize God's timetable and voice much better than in our early years. I, like Abraham, had birthed many "Ishmaels" in my attempt to help God's plan move forward more efficiently (see Genesis 16:1–3). We finally made a decision that if any commitment or initiative would send us into a frenzy of activity where we would not be able to pay attention to God, ourselves, and others, we would not do it. This became part of the way we would discern God's timing for new initiatives.

ME: Beyond my times of reading the Bible, I now needed time to pay attention to what was happening within me each day so that I could bring that to God also. Rather than keeping busy to avoid my inner pain and disappointments, I needed space to explore my feelings and wrestle with anger, shame, bitterness, grief, jealousy, fear, or depression—in an open, contemplative way before God. I began to journal what I felt as I interacted with people and circumstances throughout a day. In the beginning, my "feeling muscles" were so weak I had difficulty distinguishing anger from sadness from fear—or sometimes feeling anything at all. Over time, however, I grew in my awareness of what was going on internally within me and integrated that into the larger issue of discerning God's will. And finally, I began to listen to the gift of limits God gave me—limits related to my personality, temperament, gift mix, and physical, emotional, and spiritual capacity. This opened up for me a new world of surrendering and trusting God in the midst of obstacles and challenges.[9]

In a culture as frenetic and inattentive as ours, a "slowed down" Christian who is a contemplative presence to God and others is an extraordinary gift.

2. The Gift of Anchoring in God's Love

Christianity is not about our disciplined pursuit of God, but about God's relentless pursuit of us—to the point of dying on a cross for us that we might become his friends. The inexhaustible God loves us so intensely that every time we turn to him after wandering from his love for us, all heaven breaks out in a thunderous celebration (see Luke 15:7).

Most of us believe this intellectually. This is the message of the Bible from Genesis to Revelation. Experiencing this infinite love in our hearts, however, is another matter.

EMOTIONAL HEALTH

The sinister voices of the surrounding world and our pasts are powerful. They repeat the deeply held negative beliefs we may have learned in our families and cultures growing up[10]:

- I am a mistake.
- I am a burden.
- I am stupid.
- I am worthless.
- I am not allowed to make mistakes.
- I must be approved of by certain people to feel okay.
- I don't have the right to experience joy and pleasure.
- I don't have the right to assert myself and say what I think and feel.
- I don't have a right to feel.
- I am valued based on my intelligence, wealth, and what I do, not for who I am.

It is astounding how so many deeply committed followers of Jesus would affirm that the preceding statements articulate how they truly feel about themselves. Like the prodigal son, they are content to relate to God as hired servants rather than enjoy the full privileges of sons and daughters of our heavenly Father (see Luke 15:11–21).

Emotional health uniquely positions us to gain a small glimpse into "how wide and long and high and deep is the love of Christ, and to [experientially] know this love that surpasses knowledge" (Ephesians 3:18–19). That small glimpse alone is enough to ground us in our true identity—to know we are deeply loved by God. Because of this, we can have new, more biblical self-understanding:

- I hold myself in high regard despite my imperfections and limits.
- I am worthy to assert my God-given power in the world.
- I am entitled to exist.
- It is good that I exist.
- I have my own identity from God that is distinct and unique.
- I am worthy of being valued and paid attention to.
- I am entitled to joy and pleasure.
- I am entitled to make mistakes and not be perfect.

Emotional health powerfully anchors me in the love of God by affirming that I am worthy of feeling, worthy of being alive, and lovable even when I am brutally honest about the good, the bad, and the ugly deep beneath the surface of my iceberg.

I meet many people afraid to feel; they are worried it will unleash a torrent of negative thoughts from within themselves. They are fearful that rage, hate, bitterness, sadness, or self-doubt will erupt. Perhaps that's true. But an amazing by-product of the emotional-health journey is a fresh discovery of the mercy of God in the gospel. Not only does God not reject or punish us for being honest and transparent about our whole selves, but he actually accepts and loves us where we are. We are anchored in God's love as he gives us permission to express ourselves—the bad along with the good—and take care of ourselves in an appropriate way.

Emotionally healthy discipleship affirms that I am not a machine who simply "gets things done for God" but a human being worthy of care and rest. Emotional health connects me to the love of God, showing me that as I assert my true self and become my own unique person in Christ I do not die. It also teaches me how to receive God's love through human love and touch. Defensive walls I have built to keep other people away from me begin to crumble. In fact, learning the skills of emotional health has been one of the ways I have experienced God's glory in my marriage with Geri. I have also been able to enter into a level of unconditional, *agape* love with others that has been nothing short of a taste of heaven.

CONTEMPLATIVE SPIRITUALITY

The contemplative tradition and disciplines, then, add to our anchoring of emotional health by providing a means to keep us aware and conscious of God's love all through the day. Contemplative spirituality moves us along toward a more mature relationship with God. We progress from the "give me, give me, give me" attitude of a small child to a more mature way of relating where we delight in being with God as our "Abba Father" (see Romans 8:15–17). The progression of this movement can be broken down as follows:

- Talking at God—This is simply parroting what our parents or authorities told us to pray. (e.g., "Bless me, Lord, for these thy gifts, which we are about to receive through Christ our Lord. Amen.")
- Talking to God—We become more comfortable finding our own words to speak to God rather than the ready-made prayers of our childhoods. (e.g., "Give me, give me, give me more, O God.")
- Listening to God—At this point we begin to listen to God, and we have a two-way relationship with him.
- Being with God—Finally, we simply enjoy being in the presence of God who loves us. This is far more important than any particular activity we might do with him. His presence makes all life fulfilling.[11]

The practices of contemplative spirituality—silence, solitude, the Daily Office, meditation on Scripture, prayer, Sabbath—enable us to tune in to the awareness of God's inexhaustible love of us. They help us stop! These devotional practices are times of centering, focusing on God so that we can be mindful of his presence in times of full activity throughout the day. The Sabbath practice of truly stopping one day each week to rest, to delight in God's creation and to take care of myself, anchors me in the practice of "being," not simply "doing," every seven days (see chapter 8). Stopping for God at repeated intervals during each day—the Daily Office—also provides the rhythm to enable me to commune with him all through the day (also in chapter 8). Mother Teresa of Calcutta required her Missionaries of Charity to spend three one-hour blocks of time a day for prayer to sustain their love for the dying. Saint Francis of Assisi left the cloistered monasteries for the streets to proclaim Christ, but had a rhythm of leaving the cities to be alone with God for days and weeks at a time.

We may not be called to be monks, but we can learn many things from them as we seek to follow Christ in the twenty-first century. We each have, I believe, a solitary, a monk, within us. This is that part of us that needs rich, creative, and nurturing time alone with ourselves and with God. Emotional health and contemplative spirituality enable the "contemplative" circle of our lives to grow larger and to balance off the amount of activity in which we are engaged. This adjustment has the capacity to lead us to an incredible transformation with the love of God in each day.

One of the rich fruits of anchoring ourselves in the inexhaustible love of God is that God heals our image of who he is. Sadly, some of us relate to God as a celestial watchmaker. We live as if God created the world and set it in motion, but he doesn't really have any direct, immediate involvement any longer. So why pray?

Others of us relate to God as if he were an angry deity, consistently frustrated with us: "You're not good enough." "You are so far from where you need to be." "How can I be happy with you when you are not doing all I want?"

For still others, God is demanding and anti-human, doing what he wants at our expense. We are like helpless pawns in a chess game and God is making all the moves. Again, why pray?

Scripture reveals our heavenly Father as one who seeks our good in any and every situation. He seeks to mature us into adult children. Jesus himself said, "I no longer call you servants. . . . Instead, I have called you friends" (John 15:15). Brennan Manning summarizes well the result of regularly anchoring in the love of God:

> It is always true to some extent that we make our images of God. It is even truer that our image of God makes us. Eventually we become like the God we image. One of the most beautiful fruits of knowing the God of Jesus is a compassionate attitude towards ourselves. . . . This is why Scripture attaches such importance to knowing God. Healing our image of God heals our image of ourselves.[12]

There is, perhaps, nothing more pleasurable and healing than to be delighted by someone, especially if that someone is a God who loves us with inexhaustible love and with no strings attached. For this reason, Bernard of Clairvaux referred to Jesus as "honey to the mouth, music to the ear, and joy to the heart."

3. The Gift of Breaking Free from Illusions

The world is filled with illusions and pretense. We convince ourselves that we cannot live without certain earthly pleasures, accomplishments, and relationships. We become "attached" (or "addicted," to use a contemporary word). We attach our wills to the belief that something less than God will satisfy us. We think if we just accomplish that one big goal, then we will really feel content and good about ourselves. We will be "finished" and able to rest.

But slowly we find the accumulation of things—clothes, new electronic toys, cars, houses—no longer gives us the initial "rush" it once did. The great feeling wears off, so we convince ourselves we need more. We are seduced by the false gods of status, attention, and fame. We fall captive to the illusion that if we just get a few more words of praise from a few more important people, it will somehow be enough.

Contemplative spirituality and emotional health give us perspective on the limits of all earthly pleasures, relationships, and accomplishments. They ground us each day in reality, in God, giving us proper perspective lest the all-encompassing power of the beast overwhelm us.

At the end of the third century in the deserts of Egypt, North Africa, an extraordinary phenomenon occurred. Christian men and women began to flee the cities and villages of the Nile Delta to seek God in the desert. They discerned there was so much of the world in the church that they had to pursue God in a radical way by moving to the desert. These desert dwellers became known as the first Christian hermits. Shortly thereafter, they organized themselves into monastic communities. They saw the world:

> as a shipwreck from which each single individual man had to swim for his life. . . . These were men who believed that to let oneself drift along, passively accepting the tenets and values of what they knew as society, was purely and simply a disaster. . . . They knew they were helpless to do any good for others as long as they floundered about in the wreckage. But once they got a foothold on solid ground, things were different. Then they had not only the power but even the obligation to pull the whole world to safety after them.[13]

The call of emotionally healthy spirituality is a call to a radical, countercultural life. It is a call to intentionality, rhythm, and expectation of a life transformed by the risen Christ with the power to see through the illusions and pretense of our world.

EMOTIONAL HEALTH

In emotional health:

- I break free to live in the truth. I stop pretending to myself, to others, and to God about what is truly taking place inside me.
- I break free by choosing to live the unique life God has given

me. I no longer live the lie of someone else's life or journey.

- I break free by acknowledging my brokenness and vulnerabilities rather than trying to cover them over. I rediscover God's mercy and grace.
- I break free from the need to attach myself to accomplishments, things, or people's approval to feel okay about myself. I experience the gift of being Abba's child.
- I break free from the generational patterns of my family and culture that negatively shape how I relate and live today.
- I break free from the illusion that there is something richer, more beautiful, than the gift of loving and being loved.

CONTEMPLATIVE SPIRITUALITY

Contemplative spirituality, in addition to deepening all the above truths in our lives, adds a few others:

- I break free, on a new level, from layers of my "false self" that I am shedding so that my authentic self in Christ might emerge.
- I break free by realizing things are not as they appear to be. The idols in my life are smashed as the illusion of what they promise is exposed. I get perspective on my life in Christ over and against success as defined by the world.
- I break free from the illusion that I will live forever. Contemplative spirituality keeps the shortness of my earthly life as well as the reality of eternity before me each day.
- I break free from selfish desires that consistently move me away from God to do my own will, not his.

Allow me to illustrate how the tools of *both* emotional health and contemplative spirituality are essential to truly break free from our illusions. I worked on my family history and its impact on my present relationships for years. While in an advanced program in marriage and family, my class was given the assignment of interviewing every living member of our families. We were to put together the jigsaw puzzle of our families, uncover secrets, and understand ourselves more accurately within the context of our families. God used that experience in a wonderful way in my life to make me aware of numerous generational patterns that negatively impacted my relationship with Geri, our daughters, my coworkers at New Life Fellowship, and myself. By the power of the Holy Spirit, I was able to make specific positive changes for Christ.

Two years later, during a lengthy time of silence and solitude (one of the gifts of contemplative spirituality), I found anger at God rising up within me. I found myself angry and yelling at God! I cursed him. I called him a liar. "Your yoke is not easy and light!" I screamed aloud. (Don't worry. I was by myself.) I wondered where this was coming from.

This led me to weeks of meditating and pondering Jesus' invitation: "Come to me, all you who are weary and burdened, and I will give you rest. . . . For my yoke is easy and my burden is light" (Matthew 11:28, 30). Over time, I realized that underneath my preaching countless sermons on God's grace and love, I perceived God as a perfectionist—a demanding, hard taskmaster. But was it really him? Or was it a past I was unwilling to look at?

I came to realize during this time of solitude that the god I was serving reflected my earthly parents more than the God of Scripture. "It was never enough," was how I often felt in my family growing up. Almost unconsciously, I had transferred that to my heavenly Father with him saying, "It is never enough, Pete." I had never made that connection before.

I was stunned!

The point is simple: there are powerful spiritual breakthroughs that can take place deep below the surface of our iceberg when the riches of *both* contemplative spirituality *and* emotional health are joined together. I have seen this again in my own life and the lives of countless others. Together they form a furnace where God's love burns away what is false and unreal and where the force of his fierce and purifying love sets us free to live in the truth of Jesus.

DAVID: A MODEL OF EMOTIONAL HEALTH AND CONTEMPLATIVE INTEGRATION

The practices of contemplative spirituality provide a "container," a boundary, so that Jesus continues as the beginning, the middle, and the end of our lives. Thus the practices of emotional health never lead us to a self-absorbed narcissism; they lead us to Christ.

David, a man after God's own heart, modeled beautifully for us the seamless integration of a full emotional life with a profound contemplative life with God, writing:

> Listen to my prayer, O God,
> do not ignore my plea;
> hear me and answer me.
> My thoughts trouble me and I am distraught. . . .
> My heart is in anguish within me;
> the terrors of death assail me.
> Fear and trembling have beset me;
> horror has overwhelmed me. . . .
> But I call to God,
> and the LORD saves me.
> Evening, morning and noon
> I cry out in distress,
> and he hears my voice. (Psalm 55:1–2, 4–5, 16–17)

I invite you, in the next chapter, to come with me for an exciting journey on the eight pathways of emotionally healthy spirituality. We will begin by looking at the essential first step of knowing yourself so that you may know God.

O Lord, slow me down that I might pay attention to you through this day, that I might meet you even as I read these pages. It is safe to walk with you whether or not I feel like it today. You are a secure place. Anchor me to you today, O Lord, amidst the storms and trials going on around me now. Break me free from all thoughts and ideas about you that are not true. Unleash a spiritual revolution in my interior, Lord Jesus. Set me truly free, O Lord, that I may be a gift to those around me. In Jesus' name, amen.

PART TWO

THE PATHWAY TO EMOTIONALLY HEALTHY SPIRITUALITY

CHAPTER FOUR

KNOW YOURSELF THAT YOU MAY KNOW GOD

Becoming Your Authentic Self

Awareness of yourself and your relationship with God are intricately related. In fact, the challenge to shed our "old false" self in order to live authentically in our "new true" self strikes at the very core of true spirituality.

St. Paul, the apostle, expressed this as, "to put off your old self . . . and to put on the new self, created to be like God in true righteousness and holiness" (Ephesians 4:22, 24).

Augustine wrote in *Confessions*, in A.D. 400, "How can you draw close to God when you are far from your own self?" He prayed: "Grant, Lord, that I may know myself that I may know thee."

Meister Eckhart, a Dominican writer from the thirteenth century, wrote, "No one can know God who does not first know himself."[1]

St. Teresa of Avila wrote in *The Way of Perfection*: "Almost all problems in the spiritual life stem from a lack of self-knowledge."

John Calvin in 1530 wrote in his opening of his *Institutes of the Christian Religion*: "Our wisdom . . . consists almost entirely of two parts: the knowledge of God and of ourselves. But as these are connected together by many ties, it is not easy to determine which of the two precedes and gives birth to the other."[2]

The vast majority of us go to our graves without knowing who we are. We unconsciously live someone else's life, or at least someone else's expectations for us. This does violence to ourselves, our relationship with God, and ultimately to others. The following is a personal story illustrating how dividing our knowledge of God from our knowledge of ourselves can so easily keep us at a fixed level of spiritual/emotional development.

GERI LEAVING—AGAIN

Geri walked into the living room one day as I was reading the newspaper. "Pete, I want you to know that this summer I *am* going to the New Jersey shore."

She paused, waiting for me to react.

No, you aren't, I thought to myself.

I looked up from my newspaper and gave her an intimidating glare.

She didn't flinch.

"I'm going to live at my mother's house for the month of July. . . . I leave in two weeks."

"You can't," I said firmly. I then raised my voice, hoping to intimidate her.

"You can't leave me alone all month by myself here in New York. It will wreck our marriage."

That was not true and I knew it. I was more concerned about being lonely, about looking foolish before others in the church. We had lived in densely populated Queens, New York City, for the previous ten years.

Geri was well prepared.

"For ten years I've wanted to go down to the beach during this horrific summer heat. My mom's house is three blocks from the ocean. I've given in to your objections for ten years. I'm done. This is your issue . . . your problem. This is about you.

"I'm going," she quietly uttered, turning from me toward the kitchen.

My body screamed. I could feel my stomach knotting. My fingers formed into a fist. My neck and shoulders tightened.

This was not a discussion. It felt like a divorce.

I followed her into the kitchen. All the biblical arguments I had used the past ten years to keep Geri in New York raced through my mind:

God wants us together. One flesh . . . doing everything together. That's a great marriage.

It would be a bad witness to others. I'm senior pastor of the church. You're the pastor's wife. We are in this together . . . a team. God called us both here.

Women don't make these kinds of decisions without their husbands—or at least their agreement. This is unbiblical.

I shut my mouth without uttering an argument. I knew these simply camouflaged the true reasons why her spending four weeks in July at her mom's felt like four years and a divorce.

Geri had transformed the power dynamic of our marriage a year and a half earlier when she quit the church I pastored. This launched us into a crisis and the life-transforming journey of emotionally healthy spirituality.

She was back at New Life. Our marriage was doing well. We were babies on this new journey—together, I thought.

Why another bombshell?

She was right. It was my issue. I knew it—intellectually at least. My emotions, however, were screaming.

We had four girls: Maria, age twelve; Christy, age ten; Faith, age seven; and Eva, age three. We lived on the first floor of a two-family, semi-attached house commonly referred to as a railroad apartment (meaning the rooms followed each other like railroad cars).

I used to wake up on summer mornings and jokingly say to Geri: "Listen to the sounds outside. [We could hear the cars from a busy six-lane highway only one block away.] Just close your eyes and imagine that is the surf pounding the beach."

She rarely found the comparison funny.

What was the hard truth from which I was running, buried deep beneath the surface of my life? There was more than one.

I wanted her to be the mom I'd never had—to not "abandon" me emotionally, to be there for the "wounded boy" inside her husband who was carrying out this great responsibility for God and our family.

I also was concerned about what others thought of me. I could already imagine my Italian-American mother's reaction. Already Geri had broken many gender role expectations that had been passed on to me from generation to generation.

In my mind, I was already role-playing a conversation with my mother, in which she uttered in disbelief: "I have never heard of such a thing. I would never have done such a thing to my husband. Would never have dreamed of it!"

This was going to be way outside the box of generations of Scazzeros.

Our conversation was short that first day.

I pouted. I sulked. I grew depressed.

But I knew she was right. This was great for her, for our four girls—and ultimately even for me. But I was a big, emotional baby, depending on her in inappropriate ways, reluctant to grow up.

What is really sad is that I was leading and pastoring a large church!

I eventually stopped pouting. Over the next two weeks, we talked. Geri recognized the importance and value of our marriage, that it wasn't good to be apart unnecessarily. Between her coming back to church on Sundays and my going down to the shore for my days off, it really was only four days a week apart. That helped on one level.

Nonetheless, I struggled. And Geri went anyway.

I hated it. She loved it.

Over time, however, I grew to enjoy the time alone also. God used it to "rewire my insides," repair some of the damage from my family of origin, and help me grow into my own person apart from Geri.

It turned out to be liberating.

The reality, however, was that my discipleship and spirituality had addressed neither my insecurities nor my understanding of myself. Breaking free would require learning to feel, learning to distinguish feeling and thinking, and finally, summoning the courage to follow my God-given "true self" rather than the voices and demands around me.

FEELINGS AND THE BEGINNING OF A REVOLUTION

Like most Christians today, I was taught that feelings are unreliable and not to be trusted. They go up and down and are the last thing we should be attending to in our spiritual lives. But that's an incorrect view.

Daniel Goleman, the author of *Emotional Intelligence*, defined *emotion* as "referring to a feeling and its distinctive thoughts, psychological and biological states, and range of propensities to act." What he meant is that God created human beings to feel a wide range of emotions. There are hundreds of emotions, each with their variations, blends, and hundreds of particular nuances. Researchers have classified them into eight main families:

- anger (fury, hostility, irritability, annoyance)
- sadness (grief, self-pity, despair, dejection, loneliness)
- fear (anxiety, edginess, nervousness, fright, terror, apprehension)
- enjoyment (joy, relief, contentment, delight, thrill, euphoria, ecstasy)
- love (acceptance, trust, devotion, adoration)
- surprise (shock, amazement, wonder)
- disgust (contempt, scorn, aversion, distaste, revulsion)
- shame (guilt, remorse, humiliation, embarrassment, chagrin)[3]

It never entered my mind that God might be speaking to me in the "feeling" realm in a way that did not compromise his truth. How could I listen to my desires, dreams, likes, and dislikes? Wouldn't they potentially take me the way of rebellion, away from God?

So I ignored them.

As I said in the previous chapter, most Christians do not think they have permission to consider their feelings, to name them, or express them openly. This applies especially to when we reflect on the more "difficult" feelings of fear, sadness, and anger. It was anger and depression, however, that finally got me to stop and admit something was desperately wrong. I could no longer stuff them. I began "leaking" all over my relationships at work and at home.

When we deny our pain, losses, and feelings year after year, we become less and less human. We transform slowly into empty shells with smiley faces painted on them. Sad to say, that is the fruit of much of our discipleship in our churches. But when I began to allow myself to feel a wider range of emotions, including sadness, depression, fear, and anger, a revolution in my spirituality was unleashed. I soon realized that a failure to appreciate the biblical place of feelings within our larger Christian lives has done extensive damage, keeping free people in Christ in slavery.

OUR GOD FEELS

The journey of genuine transformation to emotionally healthy spirituality begins with a commitment to allow yourself to feel. It is an essential part of our humanity and unique personhood as men and women made in God's image.

Scripture reveals God as an emotional being who feels—a Person. Having been created in his image, we also were created with the gift to feel and experience emotions. Consider the following:

- "God *saw that it was good . . . very good*" (Genesis 1:25, 31). In other words, God delighted, relished, beamed with delight over us.
- "The LORD was *grieved* that he had made man on the earth, and his heart was *filled with pain*" (Genesis 6:6).
- "I, the LORD your God, am a *jealous* God" (Exodus 20:5).
- "For a long time I have kept silent, I have been quiet and held myself back. But now, like a woman in childbirth, *I cry out, I gasp and pant*" (Isaiah 42:14).
- "The *fierce anger* of the LORD will not turn back until he fully accomplishes the purposes of his heart" (Jeremiah 30:24).
- "I have *loved you with an everlasting love; I have drawn you with loving-kindness*" (Jeremiah 31:3).
- "How can I hand you over, Israel? . . . My heart is changed within me; all my *compassion is aroused*" (Hosea 11:8).

- "He began to *be sorrowful and troubled*. Then he said to them, 'My soul is *overwhelmed with sorrow* to the point of death'" (Matthew 26:37–38).
- "He looked around them in *anger and, deeply distressed* at their stubborn hearts, said to the man, 'Stretch out your hand'" (Mark 3:5).
- "At that time Jesus, *full of joy* through the Holy Spirit" (Luke 10:21). (Emphasis mine throughout)

Take a few minutes and reflect on the implications of our God feeling. You are made in his image. God thinks. You think. God wills. You will. God feels. You feel. You are a human being made in God's likeness. Part of that likeness is to feel.

At the very least, the call of discipleship includes experiencing our feelings, reflecting on our feelings, and then thoughtfully responding to our feelings under the lordship of Jesus.

YOU FEEL—EVEN IF YOU ARE UNAWARE OF IT

The problem, however, is that we can't reflect and respond thoughtfully to our feelings if we don't know what they are. So much of our true selves is buried alive—sadness, rage, anger, tenderness, joy, happiness, fear, depression. Yet God designed our bodies to respond physiologically to those in the world around us.

God speaks to us through a knot in the stomach, muscle tension, trembling and shaking, the release of adrenaline into our bloodstream, headaches, and a suddenly elevated heart rate. God may be screaming at us through our physical body while we look for (and prefer) a more "spiritual" signal. The reality is that often our bodies know our feelings before our minds.

When I speak about the need to pay attention to our emotions, I often hear comments such as these:

- I am not very good at feelings. I really don't have time for this. Anyway, my family was more about doing.
- I don't know what I'm feeling. It's all a big blur.

- At times when I am about to interact with authority figures or somebody I don't know, I get physical sensations but I don't know why it is happening.
- Sometimes I am flooded by emotions that disorganize and confuse me.
- Sometimes after a difficult meeting with someone (e.g., conflict) I get depressed. I don't know why.
- Sometimes, during even a TV commercial, tears come to my eyes.
- When I am feeling bad, I can't tell if I am scared or angry.
- I carry an overwhelming feeling of being shameful, guilty, and/or defective.
- My family taught us that nice girls don't get angry and big boys don't cry.

The problem for many of us comes when we have a "difficult" feeling like anger or sadness. Unconsciously we have a "rule" against those feelings. We feel defective because we ought not to be feeling the "wrong" things. We then lie to ourselves, sometimes convincing ourselves that we aren't feeling anything because we don't think we should be feeling it. We shut down our humanity.

So it was with me. I never really explored what I was feeling. I was not prepared to be honest about them with God or myself. As a result I often said one thing with my words, but my tone of voice, facial expressions, and body posture said another. The problem is that when we neglect our most intense emotions, we are false to ourselves and close off an open door through which to know God.

I remember the awkwardness when I began to be honest about my feelings. Initially I wondered if I was betraying God or leaving Christianity. I feared that if I opened Pandora's box, I would get lost in a black hole of unresolved emotions. I was breaking an unspoken commandment of my family and my church tradition.

To my surprise, God was able to handle my wild emotions as they erupted after thirty-six years of stuffing them. I came alive like never before. And I rediscovered his love and grace—much like David, Job, and Jeremiah. I also began the journey to know myself that I might know God.

DISCOVERING GOD'S WILL AND YOUR EMOTIONS

It wasn't till later that I began to learn of Ignatius of Loyola, the founder of the Jesuits, and his classic work on the importance of maintaining a balance between our reason (intellect) and feelings (heart). His development of a set of guidelines that respected the important place of our emotions in discerning God's will has served believers for 450 years. He rightly emphasized the foundation of a complete commitment to do God's will, follow Scripture, and seek wise counsel. Yet, in addition, he provided excellent guidelines for sorting out how God speaks to us through the raw material of our emotions. The issue is not, by any means, to blindly follow our feelings, but to acknowledge them as a *part* of the way God communicates to us.

Ignatius explored the difference between consolations (those interior movements and feelings that bring life, joy, peace, and the fruit of the Spirit) and desolations (that which brings us "death," inner turmoil, disquiet, and "spiritual turbulence").[4] With this inner awareness of what we are feeling in our insides, Ignatius echoed the apostle John, who said "do not believe every spirit, but test the spirits to see whether they are from God" (1 John 4:1). Sometimes they are our fleshly desires or the enemy. Other times God is prodding us to a better choice. God intends that we mature in learning to recognize how he speaks and guides us through our feelings.

One of our greatest obstacles in knowing God is our own lack of self-knowledge. So we end up wearing a mask—before God, ourselves, and other people. And we can't become self-aware if we cut off our humanity out of fear of our feelings.

This fear leads to unwillingness to know ourselves as we truly are and stunts our growth in Christ.

In *The Cry of the Soul*, Dan Allender and Tremper Longman summarize why awareness of our feelings is so important:

> Ignoring our emotions is turning our back on reality. Listening

> to our emotions ushers us into reality. And reality is where we meet God. . . . Emotions are the language of the soul. They are the cry that gives the heart a voice. . . . However, we often turn a deaf ear—through emotional denial, distortion, or disengagement. We strain out anything disturbing in order to gain tenuous control of our inner world. We are frightened and ashamed of what leaks into our consciousness. In neglecting our intense emotions, we are false to ourselves and lose a wonderful opportunity to know God. We forget that change comes through brutal honesty and vulnerability before God.[5]

Allow yourself to experience the full weight of your feelings. Allow them without censoring them. Then you can reflect and thoughtfully decide what to do with them. Trust God to come to you through them. This is the first step in the hard work of discipleship.

Once those "buried alive" emotions rose from the dead, I knew I could never go back to a spirituality that did not embrace emotional health. And when I finally allowed myself to begin asking, "How do I feel about the church, my life, different relationships around me?" before God and others, it released an outpouring that not only set me free but everyone around me.

THE GREAT TEMPTATION TOWARD A FALSE SELF

I have spent years meditating on Jesus' temptations in the wilderness (see Luke 4:1–13). They outline the three false identities or masks that Satan offers each one of us. And they show us the choices we, too, must make to remain faithful to our God-given unique life and identity.

Before the passage begins, we are given a snapshot of Jesus' understanding of who he is. Heaven opens. The Spirit descends like a dove. And Jesus' Father speaks audibly: "This is my Son, whom I love; with him I am well pleased" (Matthew 3:17). In other words: "You are lovable. You are good. It is so good that you exist."

Jesus has yet to perform miracles or to die on the cross for the sins of humanity. Nonetheless, he receives an experiential affirmation that he is deeply loved by his heavenly Father for who he is. This love is the foundation of his self-understanding and the root source of how he feels about himself.

Living and swimming in the river of God's deep love for us in Christ is at the very heart of true spirituality. Soaking in this love enables us to surrender to God's will, especially when it seems so contrary to what we can see, feel, or figure out ourselves. This experiential knowing of God's love and acceptance provides the only sure foundation for loving and accepting our true selves. Only the love of God in Christ is capable of bearing the weight of our true identity.

God has shaped and crafted us internally—with a unique personality, thoughts, dreams, temperament, feelings, talents, gifts, and desires. He has planted "true seeds of self" inside of us. They make up the authentic "us." We are also deeply loved. We are a treasure.

Three powerful temptations, however, threaten us. Each, in its own way, screams: "God's love for you will never be enough! You are not lovable. You are not good enough."

Temptation One: I Am What I Do (Performance)

The devil said to Jesus, "If you are the Son of God, tell these stones to become bread" (Matthew 4:3). Jesus had apparently done nothing for thirty years. He had not yet begun his ministry. He seemed like a loser. Nobody believed in him. He was hungry. What contribution had he made to the world?

Our culture asks the same question. What have you achieved? How have you demonstrated your usefulness? What do you do? Most of us consider ourselves worthwhile if we have scored sufficient successes—in work, family, school, church, relationships. When we don't, we may move harder and faster, go inward into depression out of shame, or perhaps blame others for our predicaments.

Thomas Merton, a Trappist monk and writer of the best-seller *Seven Storey Mountain*, tells of an occasion in his life:

> A few years ago a man who was compiling a book on success wrote and asked me to contribute a statement of how I got to be a success. I replied indignantly that I was not able to consider

> myself a success in any terms that had a meaning to me. I swore I had spent my life strenuously avoiding success. If it happened that I had once written a best-seller this was a pure accident, due to inattention and naiveté, and I would take very good care never to do the same thing again. If I had a message to my contemporaries, I said, it was surely this: be anything you like, be madmen, drunks . . . of every shape and form, but at all costs avoid one thing: success. I heard no more reply from him, and I am not aware that my reply was published.[6]

Merton understood how easily earthly success tempts us to find our worth and value outside of God's inexhaustible, free love for him in Christ.

Temptation Two: I Am What I Have (Possession)

Jesus was taken to see all the magnificence and power of the earth. The devil basically said to him, "Look around you at what everyone else has. You don't have anything. How can you think you are somebody? How will you survive? You're a nobody." The devil played on profound issues of fear and the source of his security.

Our culture measures our success by what we own. Marketers now spend over fifteen billion dollars each year seducing children and adolescents to believe they have to have certain toys, clothes, iPods, CDs, etc. Their very identities depend on it. As adults we measure ourselves through comparisons: Who has the most money? The most beautiful body? The most comfortable life? Often our sense of worth is tied to our positions at work—the money and perks. Who has the best education from what school, the most talents and awards, more degrees on their résumé? Who has the most attentive, handsome boyfriend or husband? The best-looking girl or wife?

A powerful example of this is found in the play *Amadeus*. Antonio Salieri is the court musician whose soul is destroyed by envy, by not possessing enough. He longs to create music for God and to be famous. He is really good. The problem is that he is not as good as Mozart, who is a genius. Mozart possesses the ability to actually compose a symphony in his head, something few people in history have been able to do.

Rather than recognize Mozart's genius and bring it to the world, Salieri is angry at God for being so unfair. Tragically, he believes Mozart is loved of God, while he is not.

I understand Salieri. To define myself as a son immensely loved by God, to find my personal worth in my Abba Father, who says of me, "You are my son, Pete, whom I love; with you I am well-pleased," apart from anything I do, is revolutionary. My culture, family of origin, and flesh tell me that only possessions and talents and applause from other people are sufficient for security. Jesus models surrender of my will to the love of the Father as the true anchor for who I am.

Temptation Three: I Am What Others Think (Popularity)

Some of us are addicted to what others think.

Satan invited Jesus to throw himself down from the highest spot of the temple that people might believe in him. At this point people did not think anything of Jesus. He was, in effect, invisible. How could he think he had worth and value?

Most of us place a higher premium on what other people think than we realize. What will I say or not say in a conversation? What school will my child attend? Who will I date? Do I tell that person he or she hurt me? What kind of career will I pursue? Our self-image soars with a compliment and is devastated by a criticism.

True freedom comes when we no longer need to be somebody special in other people's eyes because we know we are loveable and good enough.

M. Scott Peck illustrates the point through a story of meeting a classmate at his high school at the age of fifteen. The following are his reflections after a conversation with his friend:

> I suddenly realized that for the entire ten-minute period from when I had first seen my acquaintance until that very moment, I had been totally self-preoccupied. For the two or three minutes before we met all I was thinking about was the clever things I might say that would impress him. During our five

> minutes together I was listening to what he had to say only so that I might turn it into a clever rejoinder. I watched him only so that I might see what effect my remarks were having upon him. And for the two or three minutes after we separated my sole thought content was those things I could have said that might have impressed him even more. I had not cared a whit for my classmate.[7]

What is most startling in reading a detailed explanation of what goes on beneath the surface at the age of fifteen is that the same dynamics continue into the twenties, thirties, fifties, seventies, and nineties. We remain trapped in living a pretend life out of an unhealthy concern for what other people think.

THE DEEPLY ENTRENCHED FALSE SELF: INSIDE AND OUTSIDE THE CHURCH

Consider the two following examples. While only the second one claims to be a follower of Christ, the core issues in their lives are not that different. The tragedy is that for the Christian years of following Christ did not change her false self. It remained deeply entrenched and untouched by the power of the gospel.

Joe DiMaggio

One of my heroes growing up was Joe DiMaggio, a baseball player for the New York Yankees. Although he played for my dad's generation, stories and legend circulated for decades throughout my childhood and teen years. They placed him firmly as "the greatest living baseball player" of the twentieth century, a larger-than-life hero in American sports history. Crowds erupted into applause at his very entrance into a restaurant or public event. News reporters, year after year, praised his extraordinary talent in baseball as if he were a god.

A final jewel was added to his earthly crown when one of the most beautiful women of his day—Marilyn Monroe—became his wife.

After Joe's death, however, a devastating biography of his life was published.

It related in vivid detail how Joe's "image management," right up to his dying days at the age of eighty-three, was all a mask. It hid an egocentric, competitive, greedy, selfish man driven by power and money.

In *Joe DiMaggio: The Hero's Life*, Richard Ben Cramer details the "flatness" of Joe's life because of his commitment to "show nothing but a shiny surface of his own devising." Anyone who attempted to penetrate that surface was met with silence, exclusion, or rage. "The story of Joe DiMaggio the icon was well known. The story of DiMaggio the man had been buried."[8]

Who knows what negative core beliefs Joe might have carried within himself. I doubt Joe DiMaggio himself knew. However, one thing is sure: his life was both a lie and a tragedy.

What is perhaps more tragic is that so many of us who are followers of Jesus Christ also remain trapped within the layers of our false self.

Sheila Walsh

Sheila Walsh, Christian singer, writer, and former cohost of *The 700 Club* told her story of how, in 1992, her disconnected spirituality caused her to "hit the wall."

> One morning I was sitting on national television with my nice suit and inflatable hairdo and that night I was in the locked ward of a psychiatric hospital. It was the kindest thing God could have done to me.
>
> The very first day in the hospital, the psychiatrist asked me, "Who are you?"
>
> "I'm the co-host of the *700 Club*."
>
> "That's not what I meant," he said.
>
> "Well, I'm a writer. I'm a singer."
>
> "That's not what I meant. Who are you?"
>
> "I don't have a clue," I said.
>
> And he replied, "Now that's right and that's why you're here."

Sheila continued:

> I measured myself by what other people thought of me. That was slowly killing me.
>
> Before I entered the hospital, some of the 700 Club staff said to me, "Don't do this. You will never regain any kind of platform. If people know you were in a mental institution and on medication, it's over."
>
> I said, "You know what? It's over anyway. So I can't think about that."
>
> I really thought I had lost everything. My house. My salary. My job. Everything. But I found my life. I discovered at the lowest moment of my life that everything that was true about me, God knew.[9]

At times our false self has become such a part of who we are that we don't even realize it. The consequences—fear, self-protection, possessiveness, manipulation, self-destructive tendencies, self-promotion, self-indulgence, and a need to distinguish ourselves from others—are harder to hide.[10]

Living your God-given life involves remaining faithful to your true self. It entails distinguishing your true self from the demands and voices around you and discerning the unique vision, calling, and mission the Father has given to you.[11] It requires listening to God from within yourself and understanding how he has uniquely made you. Knowing your personality, temperament, likes and dislikes, thoughts, and feelings all contribute to your discovery.

John Chrysostom, the golden-mouthed preacher and archbishop of Constantinople, described our work as follows: "Find the door of your heart, you will discover it is the door of the kingdom of God."

JESUS' TRUE SELF

It seemed that almost everyone had expectations, or a false self, to impose on Jesus' life. In living faithfully to his true self, he disappointed a lot of people. Jesus was secure in his Father's love, in himself, and thus was able to withstand enormous pressure. He left his family of origin and their expectations of a carpenter's son and became an inner-directed, separate adult. As a result, he disappointed his family. At one point, his mother and siblings wondered if he was out of his mind (see Mark 3:21).

He disappointed the people he grew up with in Nazareth. When Jesus declared who he really was as the Messiah, they tried to push him off a cliff (see Luke 4:28–29). He remained self-assured in his beliefs, regardless of the outrage of the crowds in his hometown.

He disappointed his closest friends, the twelve disciples. They projected onto Jesus their own picture of the kind of Messiah Jesus was to be. This did not include a shameful end to his life. They quit on him. Judas, one of his closest friends, "stabbed him in the back" for being true to himself. But even though they misunderstood him, Jesus never held it against them.

Jesus listened without reacting. He communicated without antagonizing. Yet he deeply disappointed the crowds. They wanted an earthly Messiah who would feed them, fix all their problems, overthrow the Roman oppressors, work miracles, and give inspiring sermons. Somehow Christ was able to serve and love them, again, without holding it against them.

He disappointed the religious leaders. They did not appreciate the disruption his presence brought to their day-to-day lives or to their theology. They finally attributed his power to demons. Nonetheless, Jesus was able to maintain a non-anxious presence in the midst of great stress.

Jesus was not *selfless*. He did not live as if *only* other people counted. He knew his value and worth. He had friends. He asked people to help him. At the same time Jesus was not *selfish*. He did not live as if nobody else counted. He gave his life out of love for others. From a place of loving union with his Father, Jesus had a mature, healthy "true self."

The pressure on us to live a life that is not our own is also great. Powerful generational forces (see chapter 5) and spiritual warfare work against us. Yet living faithfully to our true self in Christ represents one of the great tasks of discipleship.

DIFFERENTIATION—LIVING FAITHFUL TO YOUR TRUE SELF

One very helpful way to clarify this process of growing in our faithfulness to our true selves in a new way is through the use of a new term: *differentiation*. Developed by Murray Bowen, the founder of modern family systems theory, it refers to a person's capacity to "define his or her own life's goals and values apart from the pressures of those around them."[12] The key emphasis of differentiation is on the ability to think clearly and carefully as another means, besides our feelings, of knowing ourselves.

Differentiation involves the ability to hold on to who you are and who you are not. The degree to which you are able to affirm your distinct values and goals apart from the pressures around you (separateness) while remaining close to people important to you (togetherness) helps determine your level of differentiation. People with a high level of differentiation have their own beliefs, convictions, directions, goals, and values apart from the pressures around them. They can choose, before God, how they want to be without being controlled by the approval or disapproval of others. Intensity of feelings, high stress, or the anxiety of others around them does not overwhelm their capacity to think intelligently.

I may not agree with you or you with me. Yet I can remain in relationship with you. I don't have to detach from you, reject you, avoid you, or criticize you to validate myself. I can be myself apart from you.

Read through my adaptation of Bowen's scale of differentiation on page 83. On the lower end of the scale are those with little sense of their unique God-given life. They need continual affirmation and validation from others because they don't have a clear sense of who they are. They depend on what other people think and feel in order to have a sense of their own worth and identity. Or out of fear of getting too close to someone and thus swallowed up, they may avoid closeness to others completely. Under stress they have little ability to distinguish between their feelings and their thought (intellectual) process.

Considering that Jesus was 100 percent true to himself, or "self-differentiated," where might you place yourself on this scale?

0..............25..............50..............75..............100

<u>0–25</u>
Can't distinguish between fact and feeling
Emotionally needy and highly reactive to others
Much of life energy spent in winning the approval of others
Little energy for goal-directed activities
Can't say, "I think . . . I believe . . ."
Little emotional separation from their families
Dependent marital relationships
Do very poorly in transitions, crises, and life adjustments
Unable to see where they end and others begin

<u>25–50</u>
Some ability to distinguish between fact and feeling
Most of self is a "false self" and reflected from others
When anxiety is low, they function relatively well
Quick to imitate others and change themselves to gain acceptance from others
Often talk one set of principles/beliefs, yet do another
Self-esteem soars with compliments or is crushed by criticism
Become anxious (i.e., highly reactive and "freaking out") when a relationship system falls apart or becomes unbalanced
Often make poor decisions due to their inability to think clearly under stress
Seek power, honor, knowledge, and love from others to clothe their false selves

<u>50–75</u>
Aware of the thinking and feeling functions that work as a team
Reasonable level of "true self"
Can follow life goals that are determined from within
Can state beliefs calmly without putting others down
Marriage is a functioning partnership where intimacy can be enjoyed without losing the self

Can allow children to progress through developmental phases into adult autonomy
Function well—alone or with others
Able to cope with crises without falling apart
Stay in relational connection with others without insisting they see the world the same

75–100 (Few people function at this level)
Is principle oriented and goal directed—secure in who they are, unaffected by criticism or praise
Is able to leave family of origin and become an inner-directed, separate adult
Sure of their beliefs but not dogmatic or closed in their thinking
Can hear and evaluate beliefs of others, discarding old beliefs in favor of new ones
Can listen without reacting and communicate without antagonizing others
Can respect others without having to change them
Aware of dependence on others and responsibility *for* others
Free to enjoy life and play
Able to maintain a non-anxious presence in the midst of stress and pressure
Able to take responsibility for their own destiny and life

DEVELOPING YOUR AUTHENTIC SELF

We are so unaccustomed to being our true self that it can seem impossible to know where to begin. Thomas Merton describes well what we so often do:

> I . . . love to clothe this false self . . . and I wind experiences around myself with pleasures and glory like bandages in order to make myself visible to myself and to the world, as if I were an invisible body that could only become visible when something visible covered its surface. But there is no substance under the things with which I am clothed. I am hollow. . . . And

> when they are gone there will be nothing left of me but my own nakedness and emptiness and hollowness.[13]

Getting to your core requires following God into the unknown, into a relationship with him that turns your present spirituality upside down. God invites us to remove the false layers we wear to reveal our authentic self, to awaken the "seeds of true self" he has planted within us.

The path we must walk is initially very hard. Powerful forces around and inside us work to smother the process of nurturing the seeds planted in each of us.[14] At the same time the God of the universe has made his home in us (see John 14:23). The very glory God gave Jesus has been given to us (see John 17:21–22). The Holy Spirit has been given to empower us that we might break free into our true selves in Christ. By God's grace we are to be the freest people on earth!

The issue then is how to dismantle the false self and allow our true self in Christ to emerge. The following are four practical truths to begin making the radical transition of living faithful to our true self in Christ.

1. Pay Attention to Your Interior in Silence and Solitude

We want to be the men and women God has called us to be—our true selves in Christ.

Yet enormous distractions keep us from listening to our feelings, our desires, our dreams, our likes and dislikes. Many people around us would like to fix, save, advise, and set us straight into becoming the people they would like.[15]

We need to be alone so we can listen.

My journey into emotionally healthy spirituality began very simply. Each day, as part of my devotions with God, I would allow myself to feel emotion before God. Then I would journal. Over time I began to discern patterns and God's movements in a new way in my life.

Initially, I wondered if I was a heretic to make this part of my prayer life. Finally I determined that what was going on inside of me was true whether I was aware of it or not.

I allowed myself to feel the full weight of my feelings, not censoring any of them. How did I feel about that critical comment a coworker had made to me while walking to our cars? Why was I angry? What was I afraid of? What was I excited about? What might be some of the depression I felt this afternoon?

I have been journaling ever since. I go back and read what I have written to review truths God told to me during that time.

This takes time. I slowed the pace of my life down considerably. From working six days a week (and about seventy hours), I slowed down to a five-day, forty-five-hour workweek. Over the years this led me quite naturally to the classic Christian disciplines of silence (escaping from noise and sounds) and solitude (being alone, without human contact). Silence and solitude are so foundational to emotionally healthy spirituality that they are a theme repeated throughout this book. We observe this from Moses to David to Jesus to all the great men and women of the faith who have gone before us.

Like you, I have countless demands pressing for my attention. With the hectic pace of our lives, the incessant noise of television, radio, computers, music, and our overloaded schedules, it is no wonder the ancient path of silence and solitude is lost to most believers in the West. But we must take the time. As the wise, old Abbot Moses said when a brother came to him for a good word, "Go, sit in your cell [a monk's room], and your cell will teach you everything."[16]

2. *Find Trusted Companions*

I don't know many people who shed many layers of their false self in order that their true self might emerge unless they have a few trusted mature companions to help them along the way. Deitrich Bonhoeffer in his classic *Life Together* warned: "Let the person who cannot be alone beware of community. Let the person who is not in community beware of being alone."[17] We are to be "alone together," a "community of solitudes."[18]

John Cassian, in the fifth century, tells the story of a man named Hero who spent fifty years living as a hermit in the desert, free from all concerns of the world. When the other hermits would gather for worship on Sabbath or feast days, Hero refused to participate lest he give the impression he was relaxing his strict disciplines for God. One day Hero discerned God wanted him to jump into a deep well as a test of his faithfulness. He expected an angel to save him but fell to the bottom where he lay half dead. His fellow monks pulled him out, trying to convince him he had not actually heard God's voice—but it was useless. Even as he lay dying, they could not convince him that he had not heard the voice of God. "He went along so stubbornly with his own deception that he could not be persuaded, even when faced with death, that he had been deluded by the cleverness of demons." His pride was too great.[19]

In this journey of emotionally healthy spirituality, we are talking about radical change at the core of our being. At least two critical forces hinder such a profound shift. First, the pressure of others to keep us living lives that are not our own is enormous. And second, our own stubborn self-will is much deeper and more insidious than we think. The possibility of self-deception is so great that without mature companions we can easily fall into the trap of living in illusions.

My trusted companions have included mentors, spiritual directors, counselors, mature friends, and the members of our small group and leadership at New Life Fellowship Church. They have each helped me pay attention to God and see through my inconsistencies. Most significant, God has used Geri, my wife, to lovingly reflect back to me who I am. The following is one very recent example.

I recently turned forty-nine years old. Shortly before my birthday, very innocently Geri suggested I use an illustration in a Sunday message that included mentioning my age.

I gasped, "I would never do that."

She looked stunned. "Why not?" she asked.

Then I blurted something out that surprised even me. "Well, you see, Geri, a year from now I will be fifty. Then ten years later I will be sixty. Eva [our ten-year-old] keeps reminding me that my hair is turning gray even now."

Her eyes widened, realizing something deep was going on.

"Well, I am embarrassed to be honest," I continued. I couldn't stop talking. I was getting more and more anxious. "Geri, the truth is I feel like I'm behind," I stammered. "I should have written this book when I was thirty-five, not at forty-nine. During my whole childhood I felt like I was behind . . . like I missed some major chunks of my life growing up . . . and I've been catching up ever since. I always feel different, kind of backwards. And I think that no matter what, I carry that with me."

Geri listened to my five-minute speech, realizing she was on holy ground. When I finished, she quietly replied, "This is pretty significant, Pete. You may want to get some time alone with God and reflect on that one."

"Sure," I answered, my head down. I left the room. I felt naked and silently hoped to be able to bury the topic.

God, of course, had other plans.

As I followed her question of why I could not admit my age freely, I was forced to acknowledge that sense of being backward and behind had long, intertwined roots reaching back from my family of origin that continued to impact me today. God was peeling off another layer of my false self (what a lifelong process!). He was peeling another layer off the onion that the true Pete in Christ might freely live.

Some of you reading this may be saying, "I don't have anyone to walk with me in this journey." Pray. Ask God for his person(s) during this season of your life. Let him surprise you. Often God seems to lead us to people who are very different from us and who are not pastors or leaders. Ask those you respect for suggestions. And pay attention to what he might be saying to you.

3. Move Out of Your Comfort Zone

Dying to your false self and allowing your true self to come out can be frightening. For some of us giving or receiving a compliment feels wrong. Others have an allergic reaction to being in the presence of angry people. For others to enter into conflict feels like death. To some asking for help feels like complete failure, and even thinking about disagreeing with a friend can send some into an evening of insomnia.

To begin to do things differently, especially in the beginning, will feel very awkward. For years I learned from leaders and consultants around the country how to lead a large, growing church. None of the training I received concerned itself with knowing myself. The problem was that running a large organization, overseeing budgets, and managing staff and deadlines and endless to-do lists crushed me. I was busy, very busy, and dying on the inside.

The true seeds God had placed within me—that which enjoyed preaching and teaching, creating, writing, contemplation with God, and loving people—struggled for space. I felt smothered. I was trapped. But this was God's will, wasn't it? Didn't all pastors of large churches manage large budgets and staff, constantly building and expanding the infrastructure of the organization?

Initially, it felt so wrong and strange to begin to think differently. I did not want to be a CEO or a manager. I longed to pastor and to live differently. Would the church then ask me to resign? Would people reject me?

The pain of living a life that was not God's for me finally was greater than the pain of change. It took years of hurting to get me to listen to God from within myself, to allow myself to ask the question, "Am I living faithfully to the life God has asked me to live?"

So I slowly changed how it would look for me to serve Christ at New Life Fellowship.

And the church blossomed.

I realized that what Rumi said was true: "Inside you there's an artist you don't know about. . . . If you are here unfaithfully with us, you're causing terrible damage. If you've opened your loving to God's love, you're helping people you don't know and have never seen."[20]

I truly believe the greatest gift we can give the world is our true self living in loving union with God. In fact, how can we affirm other people's unique identities when we don't affirm our own? Can we really love our neighbors well without loving ourselves?

For this reason the famous Hasidic story of Rabbi Zusya remains so important for us today: Rabbi Zusya, when he was an old man, said, "In the coming world, they will not ask me: 'Why were you not Moses?' They will ask me, 'Why were you not Zusya?'"

Changing the way we have lived for twenty or forty or sixty years is nothing short of a revolution.

4. Pray for Courage

When we differentiate into our true self in Christ, it is always accompanied by a reaction from those close to us. We may meet with a countermove or "Change back!" consequence from other people when we give up our old ways of behaving and living.

Murray Bowen, the originator of the term *differentiation*, emphasizes that in families there is a powerful opposition when one member of that system matures and increases their level of differentiation. He argues that even a little growth can cause a reaction in those closest to them.

In the same way, I have seen repeatedly that when anyone makes a change in themselves (becoming their true self in Christ), a few people around them often get upset.

Bowen describes the opposition in three stages:

- Stage One: "You are wrong for changing and here are the reasons why."
- Stage Two: "Change back and we will accept you again."
- Stage Three: "If you don't change back, these are the consequences" (which are then listed).[21]

At each season of our journey with Christ, whenever Geri and I have taken steps to more clearly define who we are and who we are not in Christ, there has always been a consequence. It will happen with you too. But keep making changes. Be willing to tolerate the discomfort necessary for growth. Pray for the Holy Spirit's power to continue. You are doing something that has never been done before in your history! In some cases you will be challenging deep multigenerational patterns. Expect that you may stir up some profound emotionality!

GOD AND THE SOUND BARRIER

When we choose to begin to make changes in our life, the pressure can feel like either our inner person or exterior life relationships will implode in the process. The shaking that happens in our life can be compared, I believe for each of us, to breaking the sound barrier for the first time. Both require great courage.

The year was 1947 and nobody had successfully broken the speed of sound—760 mph at sea level. There was a widely held belief of the existence of a "sound barrier," an invisible wall of air that would smash an airplane that tried to pierce the speed of Mach 1. In fact, a British plane, along with the pilot, had been blown to pieces in an attempt earlier that year to break the barrier. The plane could not sustain the pressure.

About that time, the United States Air Force was developing a project to put military pilots into space, but they first needed to punch through the sound barrier. Chuck Yeager was invited to be their test pilot. His boss, Colonel Boyd, informed him, "Nobody knows for sure what happens until somebody gets there. Chuck, you'll be flying into the unknown."[22]

The plane had the latest technology and design, but neither the air force nor the colonel could guarantee the outcome. Nobody had been there before.

In the same way, no other person has ever lived your life. You may be wondering what will happen if you engage in this journey of emotionally healthy spirituality, if you take seriously God's purpose for you to increasingly live faithfully out of the life he has given you.

After nine attempts, on October 14, 1947, Yeager finally broke the sound barrier. He wrote later about the experience: "I was thunderstruck. After all the anxiety, breaking the sound barrier turned out to be a perfectly paved speedway. . . . After all the anticipation it was really a let down. The 'unknown' was a poke through Jell-O."[23]

The point of this story is not that we live our life flying at high speeds. (My prayer is that you will slow down!) Hebrews 11 tells us that some people conquered kingdoms. Others were sawed in two for their faith. Only God knows your future. Yet you can be sure of one thing: your life, like Yeager's airplane, will shake in the process of you maturing into the person God intends. Why? The raw material of your life is unaccustomed to flying in order to break through the sound barrier. It will initially feel uncomfortable, as if the plane of your life is shaking from the pressure.

If you move forward, however, you will find that God is with you and behind you. His grace is sufficient. His power is accessible. And the unknown before you is really like poking through Jell-O.

Getting to know yourself so that you might know God is the adventure of a lifetime. You now have taken your first steps on the pathway toward an emotionally healthy spirituality. Let's go to the next chapter and explore a foundational issue of getting to know ourselves—going backwards in order to go forward.

And as Augustine prayed, "Grant, Lord, that I may know myself that I may know thee."

Lord, help me to be still before you. Lead me to a greater vision of who you are, and in so doing, may I see myself—the good, the bad, and the ugly. Grant me the courage to follow you, to be faithful to become the unique person you have created me to be. I ask you for the Holy Spirit's power to not copy another person's life or journey. "God, submerge me in the darkness of your love, that the consciousness of my false, everyday self falls away from [me] like a soiled garment. . . . May my 'deep self' fall into your presence. . . . knowing you alone . . . carried away into eternity like a dead leaf in the November wind."[24] *In Jesus' name, amen.*

CHAPTER FIVE

GOING BACK IN ORDER TO GO FORWARD

Breaking the Power of the Past

Emotionally healthy spirituality is about reality, not denial or illusion. It is about embracing God's choice to birth us into a particular family, in a particular place, at a particular moment in history.

That choice granted to us certain opportunities and gifts. It also handed to us a certain amount of what I will call "emotional baggage" in our journey through life. For some of us this load was minimal; for others, it turned out to be a heavy one to carry. In fact, some of us are so accustomed to walking with such excess weight that we can't imagine living any other way.

True spirituality frees us to live joyfully in the present. It requires, however, going back in order to go forward. This takes us to the very heart of spirituality and discipleship in the family of God—breaking free from the destructive sinful patterns of our pasts to live the life of love God intends.

FRANK

Frank works for a large corporation as a middle manager. Married with two teenage boys, Frank had been attending New Life Fellowship for over a year when he asked if we could get together. Walking into the diner the following week, it was obvious he was visibly shaken and depressed.

"Hi, Frank, what's up?" I asked.

"Pete, you'll never believe it," he erupted immediately. "Maria told me last night that she wasn't sure she loved me anymore. I asked if there was another guy. She said no, but who knows."

His shoulders slumped. He looked down to the floor and continued.

"You know I was never very good at this relationship thing, but I've done everything I could to be a good husband, a good father, a good provider. I don't know. . . . I pray. We pray. I have no idea what's happening."

They'd met in college and married soon after graduation. Frank then served as a pastor for ten years (in three different cities) before eventually going into business. He had recently been transferred to New York.

After a long silence, I wondered aloud, "Frank, what do you think precipitated this now—after being together so long?"

He pounced. "She's upset because I told her we might have to relocate again in two years. Well . . . she's always complaining, more than ever, of me being distant, emotionally unavailable, 'un-intimate'—whatever that is! She's also been really upset about my lack of involvement with the boys. It is just so hard for me! I try but then I slip back into my own world of work and church so quickly that . . . I don't know. . . . I've tried to make her happy." His voice trailed off to a whisper. "I don't know what to think. And I have no idea where to go from here."

Both Frank and Maria were raised in Christian homes. They know the Bible.

For years they have worshiped God and listened to thousands of sermons. They have attended small groups faithfully and served on their church worship team. They have gone away on Christian marriage retreats and attended leadership conferences.

Yet they are miserable.

Why?

Why hasn't a lifetime of spirituality in the church, surrounded by the truth of Jesus Christ, transformed deeply their inner lives and marriage? Where is the rich, abundant fruit of a life well lived in God?

Why are so many of us living lives with deeply entrenched parts of us apparently untouched by the power and mercy of the Lord Jesus Christ? This entire book, I hope, begins to offer an answer to this challenge.

One critical ingredient, however, relates to our need to go back in order to go forward. This can be summed up in two essential biblical truths:

1. The blessings and sins of our families going back two to three generations profoundly impact who we are today.
2. Discipleship requires putting off the sinful patterns of our family of origin and relearning how to do life God's way in God's family.

The pathway to an emotionally healthy spirituality calls for these key biblical ingredients to be central in our understanding of what it means to be a follower of Jesus.

THE POWER OF THE FAMILY

When the Bible uses the word *family*, it refers to our entire extended family over three to four generations. That means your family, in the biblical sense, includes all your brothers, sisters, uncles, aunts, grandparents, great-grandparents, great-uncles and aunts, and significant others going back to the mid-1800s!

While we are affected by powerful external events and circumstances through our earthly lives, our families are the most powerful group to which we will ever belong. Even those who left home as young adults, determined to "break" from their family histories, soon find that their family's way of "doing" life follows them wherever they go.

What happens in one generation often repeats itself in the next.

The consequences of actions and decisions taken in one generation affect those who follow.

For this reason it is common to observe certain patterns from one generation to the next such as divorce, alcoholism, addictive behavior, sexual abuse, poor marriages, one child running off, mistrust of authority, pregnancy out of wedlock, an inability to sustain stable relationships, etc. Scientists and sociologists have been debating for decades whether this is a result of "nature" (i.e., our DNA) or "nurture" (i.e., our environment) or both. The Bible doesn't answer this question. It only states that this is a "mysterious law of God's universe."[1]

Consider the following:

God, in the giving of the Ten Commandments, connected this reality to the very nature of who he is: "You shall not make for yourself an idol . . . for I, the LORD your God, am a jealous God, *punishing the children for the sin of the fathers to the third and fourth generation of those who hate me, but showing love to a thousand generations of those who love me and keep my commandments*" (Exodus 20:4–6, emphasis mine).

God repeated the same truth again when Moses asked to see God's glory: "And he passed in front of Moses, proclaiming, 'The LORD, the LORD, the compassionate and gracious God, slow to anger, abounding in love and faithfulness. . . . *Yet he does not leave the guilty unpunished; he punishes the children and their children for the sin of the fathers to the third and fourth generation*'" (Exodus 34:6–7, emphasis mine).

When David murdered Uriah in order to marry his wife Bathsheba, God declared, *"Now, therefore, the sword will never depart from your house, because you despised me and took the wife of Uriah the Hittite to be your own"* (2 Samuel 12:10, emphasis mine). Family tensions, sibling rivalry, and internal strife marked his children, grandchildren, and great-grandchildren for generations.

Family patterns from the past are played out in our present relationships without us necessarily being aware of it. Someone may look like an individual acting alone—but they are really players in a larger family system that may go back, as the Bible says, three to four generations.

Unfortunately, it is not possible to erase the negative effects of our history. This family history lives inside all of us, especially in those who attempt to bury it. The price we pay for this flight is high. Only the truth sets us free.

FRANK AND MARIA—THE CHALLENGE BEFORE THEM

For Frank, to follow Christ and do the serious work of discipleship will require him to examine the impact of growing up in a U.S. Army family that moved every three to four years. His father was frequently deployed away from home six months at a time. The strain was more than his mother was willing to bear. Eventually, she ended the marriage.

Frank, as the oldest child, filled in the gap his father vacated—at least financially. He worked hard but had a lot of difficulty with friendships. The frequent moves scarred him. He had difficulty getting close to people or sustaining long-term friendships.

He rarely spoke with his dad.

You can see where I'm going with this, can't you? But Maria also has work to do. Why was she so drawn to Frank's stability and good work ethic? Her father was an alcoholic who became a Christian when she was ten. He then buried himself into men's softball and church activities. He remained emotionally absent. Maria, an only child and often lonely, became very close to her mom. They'd been best friends for years, although her marriage to Frank was now putting strain on their relationship.

Both Maria and Frank have a wonderful growth opportunity before them. But it will involve a break with the old way of living and relating they had learned from their families. The ways of relating and thinking they embody go back not only to their parents but their grandparents and great-grandparents!

For this reason Christ said, "Unless you love me more than your mother, father, sister, brother [culture, other significant influences, unhealthy church traditions], you cannot be my disciple" (see Matthew 10:37). He knew our families are flawed and our relationships and patterns of loving are broken due to sin. Regardless of our culture, country of origin, education, social class, or age, the early messages and scripts we took in from our histories powerfully influence our present relationships and behaviors as well as our self-esteem.

ABRAHAM, ISAAC, AND JACOB

Genesis, the first book of the Bible, relates how the truth that sins and blessings are passed from generation to generation works out. On one level, the blessings given to Abraham because of his obedience passed from generation to generation—to his children (Isaac), grandchildren (Jacob), and great-grandchildren (Joseph and his brothers). At the same time we observe a pattern of sin and brokenness transmitted through the generations. Truly, more is caught than taught.

For example, we observe:

A PATTERN OF LYING IN EACH GENERATION

- Abraham lied twice about Sarah.
- Isaac and Rebecca's marriage was characterized by lies.
- Jacob lied to almost everyone; his name means "deceiver."
- Ten of Jacob's children lied about Joseph's death, faking a funeral and keeping a "family secret" for over ten years.

FAVORITISM BY AT LEAST ONE PARENT IN EACH GENERATION

- Abraham favored Ishmael.
- Isaac favored Esau.
- Jacob favored Joseph and later Benjamin.

BROTHERS EXPERIENCING A CUTOFF FROM ONE ANOTHER IN EACH GENERATION

- Isaac and Ishmael (Abraham's sons) were cut off from one another.
- Jacob fled his brother Esau and was completely cut off for years.
- Joseph was cut off from his ten brothers for over a decade.

POOR INTIMACY IN THE MARRIAGES OF EACH GENERATION

- Abraham had a child out of wedlock with Hagar.
- Isaac had a terrible relationship with Rebecca.
- Jacob had two wives and two concubines.

THE TEN COMMANDMENTS OF YOUR FAMILY

We often underestimate the deep, unconscious imprint our families of origin leave on us. In fact, my observation is that it is only as we grow older that we realize the depth of their influence. Each of our family members, or those who raised us through childhood, has "imprinted" certain ways of behaving and thinking into us. (Likewise our cultures, the media, our interpretation of events that happen to us also imprint us.) These behavioral patterns operate under a set of "commandments." Some of them are spoken and explicit. Most are unspoken. They were "hardwired" into our brains and DNA, so much so that apart from the intervention of God himself and biblical discipleship we simply bring these expectations into our closest relationships as adults.

Consider the following Ten Commandments tablet:

1. MONEY
- Money is the best source of security.
- The more money you have, the more important you are.
- Make lots of money to prove you "made" it.

2. CONFLICT
- Avoid conflict at all costs.
- Don't get people mad at you.
- Loud, angry, constant fighting is normal.

3. SEX
- Sex is not to be spoken about openly.
- Men can be promiscuous, women must be chaste.
- Sexuality in marriage will come easily.

4. GRIEF AND LOSS
- Sadness is a sign of weakness.
- You are not allowed to be depressed.
- Get over losses quickly and move on.

5. EXPRESSING ANGER
- Anger is dangerous and bad.
- Explode in anger to make a point.
- Sarcasm is an acceptable way to release anger.

6. FAMILY
- You owe your parents for all they've done for you.
- Don't speak of your family's "dirty laundry" in public.
- Duty to family and culture comes before everything.

7. RELATIONSHIPS
- Don't trust people. They will let you down.
- Nobody will ever hurt me again.
- Don't show vulnerability.

8. ATTITUDES TOWARDS DIFFERENT CULTURES
- Only be close friends with people who are like you.
- Do not marry a person of another race or culture.
- Certain cultures/races are not as good as mine.

9. SUCCESS
- Is getting into the "best schools".
- Is making lots of money.
- Is getting married and having children.

10. FEELING AND EMOTIONS
- You are not allowed to have certain feelings.
- Your feelings are not important.
- Reacting with your feelings without thinking is okay.

You can easily add to this list. What messages did you receive about parenting? Gender roles? Marriage? Singleness? Physical affection and touch? How did your family view God, other churches, other faiths? It is essential that we reflect on the messages that were handed down to us, submitting them to Christ and his Word.

A common, deadly commandment that prevails inside and outside the church is, "You must achieve to be loved." In other words, we must be competent in the context of competition—in school, sports, recreation, work, neighborhood, church—to feel of worth and value. As a result, many people struggle with an "achievement addiction." It never seems like enough. We consistently feel inferior. Many of us know the experience of being approved for what we do. Few of us know the experience of being loved for being just who we are.

Take a few minutes and ponder your family's commandments on this issue. How have they impacted you and your present relationships today? Our history has shaped our current lives profoundly. The cost of ignoring the impact of our past on our present life is costly.

God's desire for us to leave our families is similar to the desire he had for the Israelites to leave Egypt. Although the Israelites did physically leave the land of Egypt, a great deal of Egyptian culture and thinking remained in them. In the same way, we may choose to become Christ followers, but in reality we continue to follow, probably unconsciously, the commandments and rules we internalized in our families of origin.

The great problem, of course, is when our family's invisible scripts are contrary to Christ's. And when the family commandments passed on to us are so deeply imbedded in our DNA that we cannot even discern the difference the result can be tragic.

COMPARTMENTALIZATION

In 1976 I became a Christian at the age of nineteen. God then transferred me into his family—the body of Christ. While I now was a new member of Christ's family, almost everything I had learned about life had come from my original family.

The issue of discipleship now was how to do life Christ's way.

Learning how to pray, read Scripture, participate in small groups, worship, and use my spiritual gifts were the easy part. Rooting out deeply ingrained messages, habits, and ways of behaving, especially under stress, would prove far more complex and difficult.

My family, like all families, had invisible, unspoken rules that were expected to be obeyed. These included, for example, gender roles, how and when to express anger, views of race and other cultures, the definition of success, how authority was to be treated, sexuality for men versus women, marriage expectations, and views of the church. They were things I didn't want to address, and therefore going back to go forward was something I resisted strongly. Geri would ask me questions about my family past, and I would argue: "What good would it do to look back? It would be too painful. I am just so grateful to be a new creation in Christ." Like most people, I did not want to betray my family. What kind of a Christian would dig up "dirt" and secrets on his own family—especially an Italian-American one?

Looking to the past illumines the present. But make no mistake about it; it is painful.

Because so few people do the hard work of going back in order to go forward, the symptoms of a disconnected spirituality are everywhere. The compartmentalization of our spirituality from the rest of our lives becomes necessary because there is so little integration. I know. I lived that way for years.

Let's go back to Frank and his slow awakening to how his past was impacting his present.

THE PAINFUL FRUIT OF A DISCONNECTED SPIRITUALITY

In later coffee meetings at the local diner with Frank, I asked him to describe his family to me.

"Our marriage is really better than my parents', at least," he began. "My father's father was extremely abusive physically and an alcoholic. But my father became a Christian. He seemed to come out of the mess of his family. Yet he struggled his whole life with some sort of sexual addiction. I don't know what. He rarely spoke about it.

"Actually we moved an average of every three years as my dad took on different assignments for the army. So I never really developed close friends anywhere. Our family revolved around my dad. It was almost like everyone kind of tiptoed around him, fearing his anger—especially Mom. Her whole life, really, was about him. She gave up all her wants and desires for him and us kids. She died recently. But I'm not sure she ever really lived. She just kind of existed.

"So getting close to Maria was really hard for me. I wanted something better for us. But it didn't seem to bother her. She never said anything before—at least until now!"

After a few meetings Frank felt safe enough to unload a secret he had been carrying for a number of years: "I was exposed to pornography at age twelve. You can imagine living on an army base at that age. I've struggled ever since. I feel crippled by it, actually. Accountability groups, confessions, prayer lines—it keeps coming back. I don't know. Who knows? It's overwhelming."

Again there was a long pause as he waited for my reaction.

"I did some work with a counselor a number of years ago for depression but we never really got to underlying issues. The pornography addiction just grew until I left the board I was serving on. I just felt shame all over. Then I started to get some victory—at least for a while—so I went back to serve on the board."

Frank's life resembled a jack-in-the-box. While he regularly stuffed down his feelings of being invisible as a child or the feelings of being dominated by his parents as a young child, they often "popped" out in the present. Frank felt like he was betraying his parents talking so openly about their "secrets," but the pain had finally grown so great he had little choice.

Because this is not part of the discipleship or spiritual formation programs in most of our churches, it often takes a crisis to move someone like Frank, or myself, to go in this direction. I have not met anyone who wants to carry the weight and pass on their unfinished sins and baggage to their children and their children's children.

It is against this backdrop that the glory and power of the Lord Jesus offers such incredible hope.

THE GREAT NEWS OF JESUS CHRIST

The great news of Christianity is that your biological family of origin does not determine your future. God does! What has gone before you is not your destiny! The most significant language in the New Testament for becoming a Christian is "adoption into the family of God." It is a radical new beginning. When we place our faith in Christ, we are spiritually reborn by the Holy Spirit into the family of Jesus. We are transferred out of darkness into the kingdom of light.

The apostle Paul used the image of Roman adoption to communicate this profound truth, emphasizing we are now in a new and permanent relationship with a new Father. God becomes our Father. Our debts (sins) are cancelled. We are given a new name (Christian), a new inheritance (freedom, hope, glory, the resources of heaven), and new brothers and sisters (other Christians) (see Ephesians 1).

Jesus' mother and brothers arrived at a house where he was teaching, looking for him to come outside. Jesus replied to the crowd inside the house sitting at his feet: "'Who are my mother and my brothers?'" . . . Then he looked at those seated in a circle around him and said, 'Here are my mother and my brothers! Whoever does God's will is my brother and sister and mother'" (Mark 3:33–35). The church for the believer was now the "first family."[2]

In the ancient world of Jesus, it was extremely important to honor one's mother and father. Jesus demonstrated that, even while hanging on the cross. He entrusted the care of his mother to the apostle John. Yet Jesus was direct and clear in calling people to a first loyalty to himself over their biological families, saying, "Anyone who loves his father or mother more than me is not worthy of me" (Matthew 10:37).

Discipleship, then, is the putting off of the sinful patterns and habits of our biological families and being transformed to live as members of Christ's family.

This is the Christian life. God's intention is that we grow up into mature men and women transformed by the indwelling presence of Christ. We honor our parents, culture, and histories but obey God.

Every disciple, then, has to look at the brokenness and sin of his or her family and culture. The problem is that few of us have reflected honestly on the impact of our family of origin and other major "earthquake" events in our histories.

Philosopher George Santanya said it well: "Those who cannot learn from the past are doomed to repeat it." For example, perhaps your family defined success by profession or education or money. Maybe there were underlying messages that in order to be loved, cared for, or accepted you needed to *do* certain behaviors. This impacted your view of yourself (i.e., your self-esteem).

In God's family, success is defined as being faithful to his purpose and plan for your life. We are called to seek first his kingdom and righteousness (see Matthew 6:33). Everything else, he promises, will be added to us. Moreover, God declares we are loveable. We are good enough in Christ (see Luke 15:21–24).

Discipleship, then, is working these truths into our practical, everyday lives.

Sadly, when we look deep beneath the surface of our lives, most of us are not doing anything fundamentally differently from what our families did. God's intention, however, is that our local churches and parishes are to be places where, slowly but surely, we are re-parented on doing life Christ's way.

God intends that his new community of people be the place where we are set free.

This requires I recognize the sad reality that all of us bring to our new community our old "Egyptian" ways of living and relating. The following is a glimpse into how this worked out for me.

THE SCAZZERO-ARIOLA FAMILY

On the next page is a simplified genogram of my family. Genograms are a way to draw our family trees in a way that looks at information about family members and their relationships over two to three generations.

All our families are broken and marred by the effects of the Fall. Mine is no different. On the bottom right you will notice the bold "Pete." I am the youngest of four children. Geri and I have four daughters. By looking to the right side of the genogram you will see my

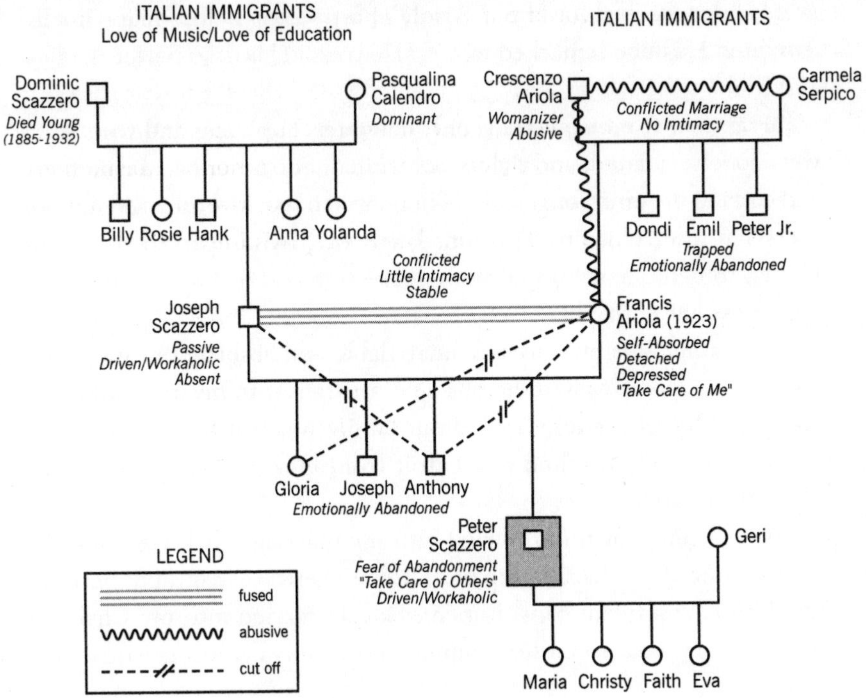

mom, Francis, with her parents, Crescenzo and Carmela, above her.

On the left side you will see my father, Joseph, and then his parents, Dominic and Pasqualina, above him.

To understand the dynamics of who I am, you have to look at my mother's family, especially the impact of her father. Her father, Crescenzo, had married my grandmother in an arranged marriage in order to come to the United States. He was a "womanizer" who lived as a "married bachelor." He sent his wife and children to work in an Italian pastry shop while he continued living his own separate life.

My mother cannot remember him ever saying her first name. Crescenzo would scream, for example: "Disgrace the family and I'll kill you." He would win a pony and give it to another man's child. When one of his friends expressed keen interest in my mom's pet dog (she was about ten years old), he gave him the dog as a gift, ignoring my mother's tears.

My dad worked for him in Ariola's pastry shop before marrying his daughter. He once remarked to me, "He treated his dogs better than his children."

Francis, my mom, was his only daughter. Her child and teen years were lonely, isolated, and tightly controlled. She never had a childhood and carried the emotional scars of her abuse into our family. Giving and receiving love, enjoying life, fun, laughter, playfulness, joy were unknown to her. She struggled with depression and feelings of profound loneliness her entire life.

My father was emotionally unavailable and absorbed in work and his hobbies. He delegated the raising of the family to my mom while he traveled. One of the tragedies of our family was that his marriage into my mom's family resulted in a cutoff from his own family that lasted more than twenty years.

What things then did I bring into my marriage with Geri and the walking out of my discipleship with Jesus? There are many, but here are five heavy "emotional bags" I unconsciously carried into my Christian life for years prior to understanding emotionally healthy spirituality.

I Over-functioned

Along with my brothers, our role was to "make Mama happy" since my dad was absent for her. Even though we were the children, it was expected we would take care of her. There was little room to play, to have fun, or to be listened to.

When I became a Christian I naturally began to take care of others. Within one year of coming to Christ, I was leading our college Christian group, taking care of the sheep. I simply transferred being overly responsible in my family of origin to being overly responsible for others' salvation and growth in the church. Is it any wonder I became a pastor to care for others? Is it any wonder that I had great difficulty maintaining healthy, appropriate boundaries as an adult?

I Over-Performed

Second, the experience of being Italian-American immigrants struggling to make it in the United States left an expectation on us: "You will make your parents proud; they have suffered so much for you to be able to succeed and go to college." The performance-based approval that ran strongly in the veins of our family now drove me to "work hard for Jesus." "Prove yourself" was the message.

We knew we were loved but always knew there was a line we could not cross. My brother Anthony, when he disobeyed my father, quit college and joined the Unification Church. He was disowned and forbidden to return home for years.

How many high-achieving, "successful" people are driven by a deeply seated shame and feeling of abandonment, silently crying out, "Notice me!"?

I Had Cultural, Not Biblical, Expectations for Marriage and Family

Third, my beliefs regarding marriage and gender roles were shaped much more strongly by my family than Scripture. Of course Geri complained. But all the women in our extended family complained about their husbands. Wasn't that normal? Our marriage sure seemed better than most. I was "helping" with the kids, wasn't I?

I never observed a joyful, intimate couple investing in the quality of their relationship before their children. Women were to stay home with the children. Men led and made the major decisions for the family. I assumed that was God's way also.

I Resolved Conflict Poorly

Fourth, even though I taught workshops on conflict resolution and communication, the basic way I handled conflict and anger resembled my family of origin, not Christ's family. My mother raged and attacked. To avoid conflict, my dad the appeaser gave in to whatever my mom wanted. I took on my father's basic style, taking the blame whenever something was wrong in order to end any tension. I justified it as being like Christ, a sheep going to the slaughter. In doing so, however, I did not love well.

I Didn't Let Myself Feel

Finally, I did not know how to accept and process my own feelings, needs, and wants. I felt "invisible" in our family growing up, consistently taking care to keep the family together. So questions such as "What do you feel? What do you want? What do you need?" were never asked to me growing up. I was naturally drawn to certain biblical teachings (e.g., Luke 9:23 on denying yourself and John 15:13 on laying down your life for others) while ignoring others (e.g., remember to rest on the Sabbath day [see Exodus 20:8]).

A child doesn't say, "What's wrong with this environment where I am growing up?" They think, *What's wrong with me?* So I grew up feeling inadequate, flawed . . . defective. *If people only knew*, I would think to myself.

I loved the message of Christ. No other religion in the world reveals a personal God who loves us for who we are, not what we do. His approval is without conditions. Yet for the first seventeen years of my discipleship the profound impact my family history had upon me blocked that truth from penetrating deeply into my experience. Like many people I meet, I lied to myself out of fear, twisting the truth to myself: *Oh, Pete, it wasn't that bad. How many people have it so much worse?*

The truth is that I did "lose a leg in my childhood." I cannot get that back. Yet because, by God's grace, I have gone back; I can walk. I may walk with a limp, but I am no longer crippled. I am free. But when I look back now and think about how I lived the first seventeen years of my Christian life, I am stunned . . . shocked . . . embarrassed. . . . There was so much needless pain!

THE PRESENT IS A WINDOW INTO THE PAST

I have examined genograms that outline the major themes of people's pasts both at New Life Fellowship Church and around North America at seminars and conferences for over a decade. Our church has people from China, Argentina, Lebanon, Poland, Greece, Indonesia, the Philippines, Haiti, India, and over sixty other countries. We've done genograms for many of them. We have done genograms for poor people from the South Bronx and suburban megachurches in the United States, for Ivy League PhDs and high school dropouts. Often people will say afterward, "Gee, Pastor Pete, I guess my family [or culture, or country] is just particularly messed up."

My answer is always the same: "No. All families are broken and fallen. There aren't any 'clean' genograms. None of us comes from perfect families with perfect parents. Most parents did the best they could with what they brought with them into adulthood. And it is likely that some of the things that did hurt us, such as criticism and rejection, were a result of what was handed to them by their families of origin rather than a reflection on us or their love for us."

Our fear of bringing secrets and sin into the light, however, drives many people to prefer the illusion that if they don't think about it, it somehow goes away. It doesn't. Unhealed wounds open us up to habitual sin against God and others.

Jane, for example, is a member of a Sunday school class. She often helps set up chairs and refreshments beforehand and cleans up when class is over. Her relationship with the primary authority figures in her life growing up—her father and mother—was strained. They were rarely home and highly critical. Also, she was abused sexually by an uncle as a teenager. Today, twenty-five years later, whenever an authority figure gives Jane suggestions or constructive criticism, she gets defensive and withdraws. She is unaware of how her unexamined past chains her to unloving, disrespectful ways of relating in the present.

The great news is that Jane can go back in order to go forward. In Christ she can emerge a freer, more whole, alive person.

You see, even the worst and most painful family experiences are part of our total identity. God had a plan in placing us in our particular families and cultures. And the more we know about our families, the more we know about ourselves—and the more freedom we have to make decisions how we want to live. We can say: "This is what I want to keep. This is what I do not want to bring with me to the next generation."

If we ignore truth out of fear, we end up like Miss Havisham from Charles Dickens's novel *Great Expectations*. The daughter of a wealthy man, she received a letter on her wedding day at 8:40 AM that her husband to be was not coming. She stopped all clocks in the house at the precise time the letter arrived and spent the rest of her life in her bridal dress (it eventually turned yellow), wearing only one shoe (since she had not yet put on the other at the time of the disaster). Even as an old lady, she remained crippled by the weight of that crushing blow. It was as if "everything in the room and house had stopped." She decided to live in her past, not her present or future.

THE BEAVER SYSTEM MODEL[3]

The Beaver System Model is one helpful, well-known way of looking at and understanding our families. Based primarily on how they understand their boundaries, families are able to classify themselves along five different levels of health.

Level Five: The Family in Pain

This is a severely disturbed family. Real leadership is totally lacking. Chaos, uncertainty, confusion, and turmoil are the adjectives that describe these homes. Conflicts are never dealt with or resolved. There is no ability to look at issues with clarity.

Level Four: The Borderline Family

This is a polarized family. Instead of anarchy, as in Level Five, a dictatorship rules here. Instead of no rules, this home has nothing but black-and-white rules. There are rigid ways of thinking, feeling, and behaving that are expected of all members. Individuals cannot say, "I disagree with what you said."

Level Three: The Rule-Bound Family

This family is not in chaos or under a dictatorship. It is healthier than Level Four. Feeling loved and good about oneself, however, depends on obeying the spoken and unspoken rules of the family. "If you loved me, you would do all the things you know will meet with my approval." There is an invisible referee, with the rules of the system being more important than the individual. A subtle level of manipulation, intimidation, and guilt permeates the home.

Levels Two and One: The Adequate Family and the Optimal Family

In these families there is an ability to be flexible and cherish each individual member while at the same time valuing a sense of closeness. Good feelings, trust, and teamwork by the parents enable members to work through difficulties and conflicts. What distinguishes Level Two families from Level One can be summed up in one word: delight. Level One families truly delight in being with one another.

Now ask yourself: Which of these five family categories best describes my experience growing up? How does my family of origin still impact me today? What are the areas I need to intentionally work on in order to move forward in Christ (e.g. boundaries, dealing with conflict, intimacy)?

JOSEPH—MODELING HOW TO GO BACK TO GO FORWARD

One-fourth of the book of Genesis is about Joseph growing up into an emotionally and spiritually mature adult who lived out his unique destiny in God. As with many families, however, Joseph's family was characterized by great brokenness and sadness.

Joseph appears in Genesis 37 at the age of seventeen, the eleventh of twelve sons and the favorite of his father, Jacob. They were a complex, blended family with Jacob, his two wives and two concubines, and all their children living under one roof.

Joseph appears immature, arrogant, and unaware of how his dreams and visions from God only further alienated him from his brothers. Their hatred of him grew to the point where they faked his death by the hands of a wild animal and sold him to Egypt as a slave, hopefully never to be heard from again.

In many ways the level and number of secrets in a family gives an indication of its level of health and maturity. Joseph's family, by that standard, was very sick. Joseph's father, grandfather, and great-grandfather all engaged in lying and half-truths, secrecy and jealousy. Now, they took this generational pattern to a new level.

Imagine the impact for Joseph. He lost his parents, siblings, culture, food, language, freedom, and hopes in one day! Then in Egypt, while serving as a slave in the home of Potiphar, he was falsely accused of rape and sent to prison for years. A door opened for his release while in the dungeon, but he was forgotten once again. He languished in prison for ten to thirteen years. What a waste! What betrayal! His life, to the age of thirty, appears to be a tragedy. If anyone should have been filled with bitterness and rage for so much family pain, it was Joseph!

Yet he remained faithful as a seeker and lover of God. Even when horrific events outside his control swirled around him, Scripture describes Joseph as "walking with God."

Then the incredible happened. Overnight, through the interpretation of a dream, Joseph was pulled from the pit of prison and made the second most powerful person in Egypt, the superpower of that day. He continued to walk with the Lord until his dying day, partnering with the God of Israel to be a blessing to his family of origin, Egypt, and the world. He honored and blessed the family that betrayed him.

Joseph went back to go forward. The question is how? What lessons can we learn from his life?

1. Joseph Had a Profound Sense of the Bigness of God

Repeatedly, Joseph affirmed the large, loving hand of God through all his pain and hardships. "It was not you who sent me here, but God," he repeatedly proclaimed (see Genesis 45:8). In doing so he affirmed that God mysteriously leads us into his purposes through darkness and obscurity. God is the Lord God Almighty who has all history in his grip, working in ways that are mostly hidden to us on earth. Joseph understood that in all things God is at work, in spite of, through, and against all human effort, to orchestrate his purposes.

God never loses any of our past for his future when we surrender ourselves to him. Every mistake, sin, and detour we take in the journey of life is taken by God and becomes his gift for a future of blessing.

Why did God allow Joseph to go through such pain and loss? We see traces of the good that came out of it in Genesis 37–50, but much remains a mystery. Most importantly, Joseph rested in God's goodness and love, even when circumstances went from bad to worse.

2. Joseph Admitted Honestly the Sadness and Losses of His Family

Most of us are resistant to going back and feeling the hurt and pain of our past. It can feel like a black hole or an abyss that might swallow us up. We wonder if we are only getting worse. Yet Joseph wept repeatedly when he reunited with his family. In fact, Scripture relates that he wept so loudly that the Egyptians heard him (see Genesis 45:2). He did not minimize or rationalize the painful years. But out of his honest grieving of the pain, he truly forgave and was able to bless the brothers who betrayed him. And he took leadership of his family to the end of his days, providing for them financially, emotionally, and spiritually. He saw how God sent him ahead to Egypt to save their lives by a great deliverance (see Genesis 45:7).

When Joseph did begin to prosper in Egypt after his long years of suffering, he gave his two children names that reflected the pain and sadness of his past. His first son was named Manasseh, from the Hebrew word for "forget," because God had enabled him to forget all his troubles. His second child was named Ephraim, from the Hebrew word for "fruitful," because God had made him fruitful in his new land of suffering (see Genesis 41:50–52).

3. Joseph Rewrote His Life Script According to Scripture

Joseph had plenty of reason to say to himself, *I don't have a right to exist. My life is a mistake. I am worthless. I should never trust anyone. I shouldn't take risks. I shouldn't feel. It is too painful. I am a loser.* Yet he didn't.

Our families and traumatic events in our histories often hand us negative messages or scripts that unconsciously direct our lives. These decisions we make, often forgotten, are replayed over and over in adult situations—even when they are not necessary. For instance, who doesn't know someone who was hurt in a church and vowed to himself, "I will never trust any spiritual leader or church again!"?

Joseph was very aware of his past. Think of a play and a script being handed to an actor for a certain part. Most of us never examine the scripts handed to us by our past.

Joseph did. He thought about it. And then he opened the door to God's future by rewriting it with God.

It has been said that the real measure of our sense of self is when we are with our parents for more than three days. At that point we need to ask ourselves how old we feel. Have we gone back to our patterns of behaving more in line with our childhood, or have we broken free from our past to live in what God has for us now?

4. Joseph Partnered with God to Be a Blessing

Joseph could have destroyed his brothers with anger. Instead he joined with God to bless them. For those of us who have been deeply wounded like Joseph, that can feel like a difficult, almost impossible path.

Joseph made a choice. It is the same choice we make every day: Is God safe? Is God good? Can God be trusted?

Joseph had clearly developed a secret history over a long period of time in his relationship with God. His whole life was structured around following the Lord God of Israel. Then when the moment came for a critical decision, he was ready. In the same way, there are the *daily* choices centered around our own walks with God (which we shall talk about in later chapters) that are critical for us to serve as an instrument of blessing to many.

ONE FINAL WORD: OUR NEED TO BE "ALONE TOGETHER"

The gravitational pull back to the sinful, destructive patterns of our family of origin and culture is enormous. A few of us live as if we were simply paying for the mistakes of our past. For this reason God has called us to make this journey with companions in the faith. Going back in order to go forward is something we must do in the context of community—with mature friends, a mentor, spiritual director, counselor, or therapist. We need trusted people in our lives of whom we can ask, "How do you experience me? Tell me the feelings and thoughts you have when you are with me. Please be honest with me." Prayerfully listening to their answers will go a long way toward healing and getting a perspective on areas of our lives that need to be addressed. Needless to say, this takes a lot of courage.

This work of going back in order to go forward for sure leads most of us to a Wall in our journey with Christ. We find ourselves disoriented, confused, and shaken by the unknown territory to which this leads. Thus, the next step into an emotionally healthy spirituality calls us to . . . journey through the Wall.

Lord, I believe you are a God with great purposes. You placed me into my particular family in a particular place in a particular time in history. I don't see what you see, but I ask you to show me, Lord, the revelation and purposes you have for me in your decision. Lord, I do not want to betray or be ungrateful for what was given to me. Yet at the same time, help me discern what I need to let go of from my past and what my essential discipleship issues are in the present that must be addressed. Grant me courage; grant me wisdom to learn from the past but not be crippled by it. And may I, like Joseph, be a blessing to my earthly family, spiritual family, and the world at large. In Jesus' name, amen.

CHAPTER SIX

JOURNEY THROUGH THE WALL

Letting Go of Power and Control

Emotionally healthy spirituality requires you to go through the pain of the Wall—or, as the ancients called it, "the dark night of the soul." For many, going back in order to go forward thrusts us up against the Wall. Others are brought to it by circumstances and crises beyond our control.

Regardless of how we get there, every follower of Jesus at some point will confront the Wall. Emotionally healthy spirituality helps provide a (partial) roadmap of both how one goes through the Wall and what it means to begin living on the other side.

Failure to understand its nature results in great long-term pain and confusion. Receiving the gift of God in the Wall, however, transforms our lives forever.

THE CHRISTIAN LIFE AS A JOURNEY

The image of the Christian life as a journey captures our experience of following Christ like few others. Journeys involve movement, action, stops and starts, detours, delays, and trips into the unknown.

God called Abraham to leave his past life in Ur at the age of seventy-five and to embark on a journey. God called to Moses from a burning bush to begin a new phase of his journey at the age of eighty. God called the Israelites to leave Egypt and embark on a forty-year journey of personal transformation in the desert. God called David to leave the comforts of his job as a shepherd to conquer Goliath and to serve as king of Israel. God called Jeremiah to forty to fifty years of difficult work, standing firm for God's values in the midst of a rebellious people.

Jesus called the twelve disciples to a journey that would change their lives forever. Judas, however, grew disillusioned and got stuck along the way. He couldn't imagine what Jesus was up to, especially in surrendering himself to the authorities to be crucified! He could not see how anything good could emerge out of the disintegration of their powerful Palestinian ministry that was helping so many people. Jesus' plan offended him.

Judas's "stuckness" eventually resulted in him quitting Christ altogether, resulting in perhaps history's saddest account of a wasted opportunity!

I meet many believers today who also are stuck. Some have dropped out altogether. Tragically, they fail to see the larger picture of the transforming work God seeks to do in them at their Wall. The disorientation and pain of their present circumstances blinds them. And they feel unsuccessful in finding other companions for such a journey.

What most don't understand is that growth into maturity in Christ requires us to go through the Wall.

THE WALL—STAGES OF FAITH

Throughout church history great men and women such as Augustine, Teresa of Avila, Ignatius Loyola, Evelyn Underhill, and John Wesley have written about the phases of this journey to help us understand the larger picture, or map, of what God is doing in our lives. In *The Critical Journey: Stages in the Life of Faith*, Janet Hagberg and Robert Guelich developed a model that includes the essential place of the Wall in our journeys.[1] The following is my adaptation of their work.

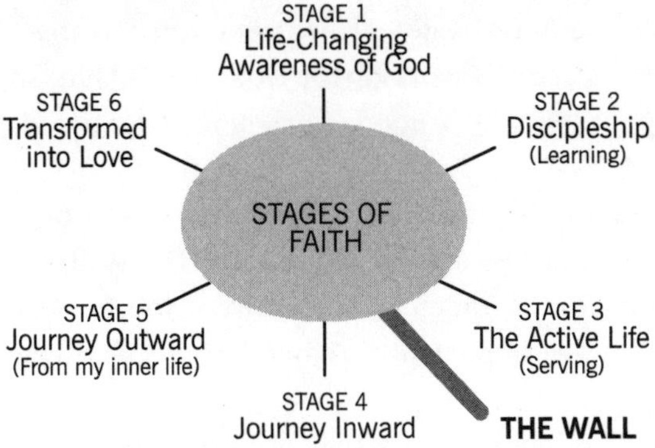

Used by permission.

Note that each stage builds naturally upon the other. In the physical world, babies must grow into young children and then into teenagers who become adult men and women. In a similar way, spiritually, each stage builds on the ones that go before it. We can't jump from the discipleship of Stage 2 to the journey outward of Stage 5.

An important difference, however, is that we can stagnate very easily at a certain stage and choose not to move forward in our journeys with Christ. We refuse to trust God into this unknown, mysterious place. We turn inward into ourselves. Our soil, ever so slowly, becomes hard (see Mark 4:1–20).

It is important to remember that while we may identify with more than one stage (I always relate to Stages 2 and 3), or even if we find ourselves in transition between them, we will still tend to have a specific "home stage that best characterizes [our] life of faith now."[2]

Let's take a look at the stages:

STAGE 1: Life-Changing Awareness of God—This stage, whether in childhood or adulthood, is the beginning of our journey with Christ as we become aware of his reality. We realize our need for mercy and begin our relationship with him.

STAGE 2: Discipleship—This stage is characterized by learning about God and what it means to be a follower of Christ. We become part of a Christian community and begin to get rooted in the disciplines of the faith.

STAGE 3: The Active Life—This is described as the "doing" stage. We get involved, actively working for God, serving him and his people. We take responsibility by bringing our unique talents and gifts to serve Christ and others.

STAGE 4: The Wall and the Journey Inward—Notice that the Wall and the Inward Journey are closely related. The Wall compels us into an Inward Journey. In some cases the Inward Journey eventually leads us to the Wall. Most importantly, remember it is God who brings us to the Wall.

STAGE 5: The Journey Outward—Having passed through the crisis of faith and the intense inner journey necessary to go through the Wall, we begin once again to move outward to "do" for God. We may do some of the same active external things we did before (e.g., give leadership, serve, and initiate acts of mercy toward others). The difference is that now we give out of a new, grounded center of ourselves in God. We have rediscovered God's profound, deep, accepting love for us. A deep, inner stillness now begins to characterize our work for God.

STAGE 6: Transformed by Love—God continually sends events, circumstances, people, and even books into our lives to keep us moving forward on our journeys. He is determined to complete the work he began in us, whether we like it or not! His goal, in the language of John Wesley, is that we be made perfect in love, that Christ's love becomes our love both toward God and others. We realize love truly is the beginning and the end. By this stage, the perfect love of God has driven out all fear (see 1 John 4:18). And the whole of our spiritual lives is finally about surrender and obedience to God's perfect will.

I prefer the notions of seasons to stages when describing our life in Christ. We don't control the seasons; they happen to us. Winter, spring, summer, and fall come to us whether we like it or not.

So do Walls.

For most of us the Wall appears through a crisis that turns our world upside down. It comes, perhaps, through a divorce, a job loss, the death of a close friend or family member, a cancer diagnosis, a disillusioning church experience, a betrayal, a shattered dream, a wayward child, a car accident, an inability to get pregnant, a deep desire to marry that remains unfulfilled, a dryness or loss of joy in our relationship with God. We question ourselves, God, the church. We discover for the first time that our faith does not appear to "work." We have more questions than answers as the very foundation of our faith feels like it is on the line. We don't know where God is, what he is doing, where he is going, how he is getting us there, or when this will be over.

My Wall included a number of events piling up one after the other. It began with a feeling of betrayal during a church split in our Spanish congregation. This was followed by a long-lasting depression and loss of motivation to serve Christ, a marital crisis with Geri, and a careful look at how my family of origin had impacted who I was in the present. I had tried to go around, jump over, and then dig a hole under the Wall. None succeeded. I finally went forward *through* it because the pain of staying where I was felt unbearable.

On a certain level it is correct to say that Walls come to us in various ways throughout our lifetimes. It is not simply a one-time event that we pass through and get beyond. It appears to be something we return to as part of our ongoing relationship with God. We see this, for example, in Abraham waiting at the Wall for twenty-five years for the birth of his first child with his wife, Sarah. Ten to thirteen years later God led him again to another Wall—the sacrificing of that long-awaited son he loved, Isaac, on an altar. Consider Moses, Elijah, Nehemiah, Jeremiah, and Paul. Each appears to have gone through the Wall numerous times in their journey with God. "Unintentionally and unknowingly we fall back into imperfections. Bad habits are like living roots that return. These roots must be dug away and cleared from the garden of our soul. . . . This requires the direct intervention of God."[3]

Note I said "gone through," not "gotten to." Because these men did make the journey to the other side of the Wall. As can we. When we make it through the Wall, we no longer have a need to be well known or successful, but to do God's will. We have now tasted what it means to live in union with the love of God through Christ in the Holy Spirit. We have learned, like the apostle Paul, "the secret of being content in any and every situation" (Philippians 4:12). We have become "whole and holy" (Ephesians 1:4 MSG). We have become, finally, our true selves in Christ.[4]

STUCK AT THE WALL—THE DARK NIGHT OF THE SOUL

Without an understanding of the Wall in the journey, however, countless sincere followers of Christ stagnate there and no longer move forward with God's purpose for their lives. Some of us hide behind our faith to flee the pain of our lives rather than trust God to transform us through it. We utter platitudes like "God uses all things for good" (see Romans 8:28). We smile and sing contemporary praise songs about our victory in Jesus. We don't curse or get bitter toward God. We keep it together to demonstrate to the weaker members of the body and the watching world that our faith is solid and strong.

The problem is that emotionally healthy faith admits the following:

- I am bewildered.
- I don't know what God is doing right now.
- I am hurt.
- I am angry.
- Yes, this is mystery.
- I am very sad right now.
- O God, why have you forsaken me?

The best way to understand the dynamics of the Wall is to examine the classic work of St. John of the Cross, *Dark Night of the Soul*, written over five hundred years ago.[5] He described the journey in three phases: beginners, progressives, and perfect. To move out of the beginning stage, he argued, required the receiving of God's gift of the dark night, or the Wall. This is the "ordinary way" we grow in Christ. A failure to understand this is one of the major reasons many start out well in their journeys but do not finish.

How do we know we are in "the dark night"? Our good feelings of God's presence evaporate. We feel the door of heaven has been shut as we pray. Darkness, helplessness, weariness, a sense of failure or defeat, barrenness, emptiness, dryness descend upon us. The Christian disciplines that have served us up to this time "no longer work." We can't see what God is doing and we see little visible fruit in our lives.

This is God's way of rewiring and "purging our affections and passions" that we might delight in his love and enter into a richer, fuller communion with him. God wants to communicate to us his true sweetness and love. He longs that we might know his true peace and rest. He works to free us from unhealthy attachments and idolatries of the world. He longs for an intimate, passionate love relationship with us.

For this reason, John of the Cross wrote that God sends us "the dark night of loving fire" to free us. John listed the seven deadly spiritual imperfections of beginners that must be purified:

1. Pride: they have a tendency to condemn others and become impatient with their faults. They are very selective in who can teach them.
2. Avarice: they are discontent with the spirituality God gives them. They never have enough learning, are always reading many books rather than growing in poverty of spirit and their interior life.
3. Luxury: they take more pleasure in the spiritual blessings of God than God himself.
4. Wrath: they are easily irritated, lacking sweetness, and have little patience to wait on God.
5. Spiritual gluttony: they resist the cross and choose pleasures like children do.
6. Spiritual envy: they feel unhappy when others do well spiritually. They are always comparing.
7. Sloth: they run from that which is hard. Their aim is spiritual sweetness and good feelings.[6]

While in chapter four I talked about the critical importance of paying attention to our feelings in order to know God, the "dark night," protects us from worshiping them. This is one of the more common idolatries of the spiritual life.

St. John of the Cross knew our tendency to become attached to feelings of and about God, mistaking them for God himself. These sensations, rich or empty, are not God but only messengers from God that speak to us of him. There is no other way, John of the Cross would say, for our souls to be strengthened and purified so that we don't worship our feelings than for God to remove them altogether.[7] This is God's way of rewiring our taste buds that we might taste of him ever more fully.

St. John wrote: "[God] is purging the soul, annihilating it, emptying it or consuming in it (even as fire consumes the mouldiness and the rust of metal) all the affections and imperfect habits which it has contracted its whole life. . . . These are deeply rooted in the substance of the soul. . . . At the same time, it is God who is passively working here in the soul."[8]

In addition to purging our will and understanding of the deadly sins mentioned above, God also adds something into our souls. He mysteriously infuses or imparts his love into us. God powerfully invades us when we persevere patiently through this suffering. Our great temptation is to quit or go backwards, but if we remain still, listening for his voice, God will insert something of himself into our character that will mark the rest of our journey with him.[9]

FINDING MY WAY THROUGH THE WALL

For many years I failed to distinguish the "dark night of the soul" from trials and setbacks. This confusion hindered me from actually going through the Wall. I surmised I had suffered more than the average Christian. That surely qualified me for undeserved blessings, didn't it?

In 1994 I was pastoring two congregations in two languages—one in English in the morning and one in Spanish in the afternoon. Life was very difficult. There were constant crises and difficulties, but they were mostly due to a discipleship that did not include emotional health.

When the afternoon Spanish congregation split and two hundred people left to start another congregation, my dark night began. I was depressed and angry. For the first time in my Christian life I did not "feel" God's presence. The Bible turned to dust. My prayers seemed to bounce back from heaven. God was not delivering me!

I thought I had hit the bottom and could only go up.

I remember telling a former member of our church about this rock bottom I had hit.

"Rock bottom," she laughed. "You have no idea how much further you have to go!"

I was in so much pain that I was incredulous at such a statement, but she seemed to discern there was some deep cleansing that was needed in me. She was right. There would be over two more years of life in the "valley of the shadow of death" (Psalm 23:4). I thought it would never end. It would take our marriage hitting the Wall and Geri leaving the church I was pastoring to finally drive me to my knees. I remember asking God, "Is there anything else you want to rip out of me, you sadist?"

For that two-year period I continued my spiritual disciplines. I followed Jesus out of obedience. I served him as a leader, but everything in me wanted to quit. Quit God and quit his messed-up church forever. Little did I know he was both purging and implanting something into my person during that horror.

I still remember coming out of it. I began to crawl and to feel for the first time, saying to myself, "Something is different. Totally different. I cannot explain it, but I feel freer than ever from people's opinions, more clear about who I am, more certain of God and his love than ever!"

I hope this means God has no other "dark nights" for me.

Biblical history seems to suggest this may not be the case.

HOW LONG WILL THIS LAST?

It may be months. More probably, it may be a year or two . . . or more.

Sorry. I know this is not what you want to read. Ultimately God chooses the length and level of intensity. He has a unique purpose for each of us, knowing how much there is to cleanse out of our inner being, and how much he wants to infuse of himself into us for his greater, long-term purposes. Our Father knows how much we can handle.

Actually, John of the Cross divides the dark night into two levels. The first level (which he terms "the night of the sense") is the one all of us encounter as we journey with Christ. The second ("the night of the spirit") is for a very few. He describes it as "violent and severe" as we "are dragged down and immersed again into a worse degree of affliction more severe and darker and more grievous . . . the brighter and purer is the supernatural and divine light, the more it darkens the soul."[10]

What is important here is to note that the trials we encounter each day are not the Wall or "the dark night of the soul." Trials are the traffic jams, annoying bosses, delayed airplane departures, car breakdowns, fevers, and barking dogs in the middle of the night.

James refers to this: "Consider it pure joy, my brothers, whenever you face trials of many kinds, because you know that the testing of your faith develops perseverance. Perseverance must finish its work so that you may be mature and complete, not lacking anything" (James 1:2–4).

Walls are David fleeing a jealous king for thirteen years in the desert. Walls are Abraham waiting twenty-five years for the birth of his first child, Isaac. Walls are Job losing his ten children, health, and possessions in a day!

CHARACTERISTICS OF LIFE ON THE OTHER SIDE

It can be difficult to discern precisely when we began the journey through the Wall and when we might be on the other side. I know many people who have been through great sufferings and hit formidable Walls. Yet the Walls did not change them. They only bounced off them. They returned to a similar, but different Wall later. Again they bounced off it, often more bitter and angry than before.

Ultimately, God is the One who moves us through the Wall. And with that comes mystery. How and when God takes us through is up to him. We make choices to trust God, to wait on God, to obey God, to stick with God, to remain faithful when everything in us wants to quit and run. But it is *his* slow, deep work of transformation in us, not ours.

So how do we know we are making progress or if we are, perhaps, even on the other side? The following are at least four dynamics to consider:

1. A Greater Level of Brokenness

Christians can be notoriously judgmental in the name of standing up for the truth. But people who have been through the Wall are broken. They have seen, as Karl Barth notes, that "the root and origin of sin is the arrogance in which man wants to be his own and his neighbor's judge."[11] Before we go through the Wall, we prefer to exercise the right to determine good and evil rather than leave this knowledge to God. Afterward, we know better.

I know. I am embarrassed when I think of how I regularly judged other people's journeys with Christ that were different from mine. I had an opinion and attitude about almost everyone who was different from me.

The first words uttered by Jesus in the New Testament were revolutionary: "Blessed are the poor in spirit, for theirs is the kingdom of heaven" (Matthew 5:3). The word he used described a beggar who had hit rock bottom, having been stripped of everything. Jesus was not describing a person in total destitution materially but one destitute of elevating themselves above others.

Picture a beggar. Not someone you might find on the streets of a North American city, strolling along looking for change to buy beer or cigarettes. Rather, picture a person in such abject poverty that he is incapable of doing anything more than lying in a corner with a palm upraised, hoping someone will take pity on him. Picture someone who knows he will die unless someone has mercy upon him. Can you imagine that beggar saying:

- I wasn't always like this; I graduated high school.
- I don't like the way you are looking at me. Keep your money.
- I earn more money than the rest of these beggars.
- Look at what that other beggar on the corner is wearing. Doesn't he have any shame?

People on the other side of the Wall are freed from judging others.

Pride and our tendency to judge others is found in every corner of the world, in all cultures, workplaces, playgrounds, families, neighborhoods, sports teams, classrooms, marriages, homeless shelters, corporate boardrooms, and ten-year-olds' birthday parties. When we become Christians it does not automatically disappear. It only takes on a new face:

- I can't believe she calls herself a Christian.
- Megachurch members are superficial.
- Their church is small and dead.
- Look at what he is doing. He is not a Christian.

Another helpful way to measure your level of brokenness is to consider how offendable we are. (Yes, I realize *offendable* is not in the dictionary). Imagine an inflated, bloated person who, when criticized, judged, or insulted, immediately pulls back and reacts. He either goes on the attack or decides we no longer exist.

Contrast that image with a broken person who is so secure in the love of God that she is unable to be insulted. When criticized, judged, or insulted, she thinks to herself, *It is far worse than you think!*

"Blessed is he who expects nothing, for he shall enjoy everything," said St. Francis of Assisi.[12] Few people enjoyed earthly things as well as him. He understood that no one can earn a star or a sunset, that gratitude and dependence on God are the very bedrock of reality. St. Francis, like others who have gone through the Wall, appreciated that we all depend, in every instant, upon the mercy of God.

That is one of the reasons I have integrated into my spiritual disciplines the Jesus Prayer. The words of the prayer, adapted from a parable of Jesus found in Luke 18:9–14, are: "Lord Jesus Christ, Son of God, have mercy on me, a sinner." Dating back to the sixth century, the Jesus Prayer has long been a foundation of Eastern Christian spirituality to help believers remain grounded and dependent on God throughout the day. By repeating the prayer throughout the day, synchronizing the syllables of these words with our heartbeat throughout the day, the intention is that our very lives will embody the richness of the prayer.[13]

2. A Greater Appreciation for Holy Unknowing (Mystery)

I like control. I like to know where God is going, exactly what he is doing, the exact route of how we are getting there, and exactly when we will arrive. I also like to remind God of his need to behave in ways that fit in with my clear ideas of him. For example, God is just, merciful, good, wise, loving. The problem, then, is that God is beyond the grasp of every concept I have of him. He is utterly incomprehensible.

Yes, God is everything revealed in Scripture, but also infinitely more. God is not an object that I can determine, master, possess, or command.[14] And still I try to somehow use my "clear ideas" about God to give me power over him, to somehow possess him. Unconsciously, I make a deal with God that goes something like this: "I obey and keep my part of the bargain. Now you bless me. Do not allow any serious suffering."

God doesn't appreciate being demoted to the rank of our personal secretary or assistant. Remember who we are dealing with here: God is immanent (so close) and yet transcendent (so utterly above and far from us). God is knowable, yet he is unknowable. God is inside us and beside us, yet he is wholly different from us. For this reason Augustine wrote, "If you understand, it is not God you understand."[15]

Most of the time we have no idea what God is doing.

There is an old story about a wise man living on one of China's vast frontiers. One day, for no apparent reason, a young man's horse ran away and was taken by nomads across the border. Everyone tried to offer consolation for the man's bad fortune, but his father, a wise man, said, "What makes you so sure this is not a blessing?"

Months later, his horse returned, bringing with her a magnificent stallion. This time everyone was full of congratulations for the son's good fortune. But now his father said, "What makes you so sure this isn't a disaster?"

Their household was made richer by this fine horse the son loved to ride. But one day he fell off his horse and broke his hip. Once again, everyone offered their consolation for his bad luck, but his father said, "What makes you so sure this is not a blessing?" A year later nomads invaded across the border, and every able-bodied man was required to take up his bow and go into battle. The Chinese families living on the border lost nine of every ten men. Only because the son was lame did father and son survive to take care of each other.

What appeared like a blessing and success has been a terrible thing. What has appeared to be a terrible event has often turned out to be a rich blessing.[16]

I, too, can honestly say that the more I know about God, the less I know about him.

Moses first saw God in a burning bush. God appeared in light (see Exodus 3:2). Then God led Moses into the desert where he revealed himself in a pillar of cloud by day and fire by night. This was a mix of light and darkness (see Exodus 13:21). Finally, God led Moses into the "thick darkness" of Mount Sinai where God spoke to him face to face (see Exodus 20:21). As Gregory of Nyssa first noted, it was in this pure darkness that the Infinite Light of God dwelled. And the more Moses grew to know God, the wilder, more dazzling, and "unknown" this true and living God became to him.[17]

Saint Thomas Aquinas in the 1200s wrote a twenty-volume work on God. He began his work: "This is the ultimate knowledge about God, to know that we do not know." At the end of his life, however, he had a vision of Christ in church. After that experience he stated, "I can no longer write, for God has given me such glorious knowledge that all contained in my works are as straw—barely fit to absorb the holy wonders that fall in a stable."[18]

One of the great fruits of the Wall is a childlike, deepened love for mystery. We can rest more easily and live more freely on the other side of the Wall, knowing that God is in control and worthy of our trust. Joyfully we can then sing with David: "He made darkness his covering, his canopy around him" (Psalm 18:11).

3. A Deeper Ability to Wait for God

An outgrowth of greater brokenness and holy unknowing is a greater capacity to wait upon the Lord. Going through the Wall breaks something deep within us—that driving, grasping, fearful self-will that must produce, that must make something happen, that must get it done for

God (just in case he doesn't).

If I were to identify my greatest sins and errors of judgment in the last thirty years of following Christ, they would each go back to a failure to wait on the Lord. What does it truly mean when we read, "Wait for the LORD; be strong and take heart and wait for the LORD" (Psalm 27:14)? Or "I wait for the LORD, my soul waits, and in his word I put my hope. My soul waits for the Lord" (Psalm 130:5–6)?

From finishing people's sentences to starting new daughter churches too quickly, I have struggled to wait upon the Lord. God, I believe, extended my Wall (and then added a few smaller ones) to purge out of me this deep, stubborn willfulness to run ahead of him. While I kick and scream, God slowly teaches me to wait. Now I understand why this is such a consistent theme in Scripture.

Abraham learned to wait at his Wall. At seventy-five years old, he was told he would be a father of nations. After eleven years of waiting, he took matters into his own hands and birthed Ishmael through his maidservant Hagar (see Genesis 16:1–4). God forced him to wait another fourteen years before the promised child was born. The public and private humiliation he suffered transformed him into a father of faith for all history.

Moses learned to wait at his Wall. After murdering a man and failing to deliver the Israelites, he spent the next forty years learning to wait on God. In the desert God transforms him into the meekest man on the earth (see Numbers 12:3).

David learned to wait at his Wall. After a stunning victory over Goliath, David, innocent, was forced to flee the mighty army of King Saul for ten to thirteen years, losing his dreams, family, reputation, and earthly security. In the wilderness God transformed him into a man after his own heart (see 1 Samuel 16 through 2 Samuel 1).

Hannah learned to wait at the Wall. After years of infertility, unanswered prayers, and mocking from the second wife of her husband, God finally heard her prayers. Her years of pain and grief transformed her into the godly mother of Samuel who would transform a nation (see 1 Samuel 1 and 2).

Jesus learned to wait in obscurity and silence, both as a lowly carpenter's son and in the wilderness, resisting the temptation of the devil to act before his Father's time. Out of this waiting Jesus emerged from the wilderness in the power of the Spirit (see Luke 4:14). We can trust God to do the same in us—if we will learn to wait on him.

4. A Greater Detachment.

The critical issue on the journey with God is not "Am I happy?" but "Am I free? Am I growing in the freedom God gave me?"[19] Paul addressed this central issue of detachment in 1 Corinthians 7:29–31, calling us to a radical, new understanding of our relationship to the world:

> What I mean, brothers, is that the time is short. From now on those who have wives should live as if they had none; those who mourn, as if they did not; those who are happy, as if they were not; those who buy something, as if it were not theirs to keep; those who use the things of the world, as if not engrossed in them. For this world in its present form is passing away.

We are to live our lives as the rest of the world—marrying, experiencing sorrow and joy, buying things and using them—but always with awareness that these things in themselves are not our lives. We are to be marked by eternity, free from the dominating power of things.

Detachment is the great secret of interior peace. Along the way, in this journey with Christ, we get attached to (literally "nailed to") behaviors, habits, things, and people in an unhealthy way. For example, I love my home, my car, my books, Geri, our four daughters, our church, our comforts, and my good health. Like you, I rarely realize how attached I am to something until God removes it. Then the power struggle begins. I say, "God I must have that second car for convenience." God answers, "No, you don't need that. You need me!"

When we put our claws into something and we don't want to take them out, we are beyond enjoying them. We now *must* have them.

The Wall, more than anything else, cuts off our attachments to who we think we ought to be, or who we falsely think we are. Layers of our counterfeit self are shed. Something truer, that is Christ in and through us, slowly emerges.

Richard Rohr has written extensively about the five essential truths to which men must awaken if they are to grow up into their God-given masculinity and spirituality.[20] His conclusions, I believe, describe the powerful biblical truths all of us can now truly know as a result of going through the Wall and experiencing a greater detachment:

- Life is hard.
- You are not that important.
- Your life is not about you.
- You are not in control.
- You are going to die.[21]

A FINAL WORD

Remember, God's purpose for us is to have a loving union with him at the end of the journey. We joyfully detach *from* certain behaviors and activities *for* the purpose of a more intimate, loving attachment to God. We are to enjoy the world, for God's creation is good. We are to appreciate nature, people, and all God's gifts, along with his presence in Creation—without being ensnared by them. It has rightly been said that those who are the most detached on the journey are best able to taste the purest joy in the beauty of created things.

Thomas Merton summed up our challenge well: "I wonder if there are 20 men alive in the world now who see things as they really are. That would mean that there were 20 men who were free, who were not dominated or even influenced by an attachment to any created thing or to their own selves or to any gift of God."[22]

The journey with Jesus calls us to a life of undivided devotion to him. This requires that we simplify our lives, removing distractions. Part of that will mean learning to grieve our losses and embrace the gift of our limits. To this we now turn in the next chapter.

Heavenly Father, teach me to trust you even when I do not know where you are going. Help me to surrender and not turn inward into myself out of fear. The storms and winds of life, O Lord, blow strongly all around me. I cannot see in front of me. Sometimes I feel like I am going to drown. Lord, you are centered, utterly at rest and peace. Open my eyes that I might see you are with me on the boat. I am safe. Awaken me, Jesus, to your presence within me, around me, above me, and below me. Grant me grace to follow you into the unknown, into the next place in my journey with you. In your name, amen.

CHAPTER SEVEN

ENLARGE YOUR SOUL THROUGH GRIEF AND LOSS

Surrendering to Your Limits

There is no greater disaster in the spiritual life than to be immersed in unreality. In fact the true spiritual life is not an escape from reality but an absolute commitment to it. Loss marks the place where self-knowledge and powerful transformation happen—if we have the courage to participate fully in the process. Loss and grief, however, cannot be separated from the issue of our limits as human beings.

Limits are behind all loss. We cannot do or be anything we want. God has placed enormous limits around even the most gifted of us. Why? To keep us grounded, to keep us humble. In fact, the very meaning of the word *humility* has its root in the Latin *humus*, meaning "of the earth."

Our culture routinely interprets losses as alien invasions that interrupt our "normal" lives. We numb our pain through denial, blaming, rationalizations, addictions, and avoidance. We search for spiritual shortcuts around our wounds. We demand others take away our pain.

Yet we all face many deaths within our lives. The choice is whether these deaths will be terminal (crushing our spirit and life) or open us up to new possibilities and depths of transformation in Christ.

THE STORY OF US ALL

Jonathan Edwards, in a famous sermon on the book of Job, noted that the story of Job is the story of us all. Job lost everything in one day—his family, his wealth, his health (see Job 1:13–2:8). Most of us experience our losses more slowly, over the span of a lifetime, until we find ourselves on the door of death, leaving *everything* behind.

We lose our youthfulness. No amount of plastic surgery, cosmetics, good diet, or exercise routine can stop the process of growing older.

We lose our dreams. Who has not lost dreams, dreams of a career or marriage or children for which we hoped?

We lose our routines and stability in transitions. Each time we change jobs, immigrate to a new country, or move is a loss. Our children grow more independent and more powerful as they move through their life transitions. Our influence and power decrease. Our parents age, and we become their caretakers.

Most of us, in one or more moments of our lives, experience catastrophic loss. Unexpectedly, a family member dies. A friend or son commits suicide. Our spouse has an affair. We find ourselves single again after a painful divorce or breakup. We are diagnosed with cancer. Our company suddenly downsizes and we find ourselves unemployed after twenty-five years of stable employment. Our child is born severely handicapped. A loyal friend betrays us. Infertility, miscarriages, broken friendships, loss of memory or mental acuity, abuse.

We grieve the many things we can't do, our limits. We experience greater or lesser losses from our families growing up. Some people, like me, "lost a leg in that war" during our childhood years and now walk with a limp.

Finally, we lose our wrong ideas of God and the church. (Thank God!) What makes this so difficult is how much we invested of our lives into a certain way of following Jesus, into certain applications of biblical truths, only to realize much of it was foolishness or perhaps even wrong. We feel betrayed by a church tradition, a leader, or even God himself. We realize God truly is much larger and more incomprehensible than we thought.

We lose our illusions about this new family of Jesus, the church. It is not the perfect family with perfect people as we expected. In fact, people disappoint us. At times, we are bewildered and shocked by their lack of awareness and sin (evil). Every person who lives in community with other believers, sooner or later, experiences this disillusionment and the grief that accompanies it.

JOB

Job was the Bill Gates of his day. His wealth was staggering. The Bible tells us he had seven thousand sheep, three thousand camels (prestigious animals in his day), five hundred yoke of oxen, and five hundred donkeys, along with a large staff of employees. In today's world, we would see Job's face on the front page of *Forbes* magazine each year for being the richest person in the world. His assets would include a fleet of Rolls-Royces and Lexuses, private airplanes, impressive yachts, thriving businesses, and expansive real-estate holdings. "He was the greatest man among all the people of the East" (Job 1:3).

Job was also very godly, faithfully walking with God, delighting and obeying him with all his heart. "He feared God and shunned evil" (Job 1:1b). Today we would say he was one of the most well-known, respected Christian leaders of our day.

Suddenly, all the forces of heaven and earth, from the east, west, north, and south, came against Job. Enemies invaded. Lightening struck. A tornado unleashed her fury. By the end of the afternoon, the unthinkable had happened—the world's richest man had been reduced to poverty and his ten children had been killed in a terrible natural disaster.

Amazingly, Job neither sinned nor blamed God. He responded beautifully; he worshiped.

Then, as he attempted to get on his feet, Job's body was seized with "sore boils" from the soles of his feet to the top of his head. His skin darkened and shriveled. His sores became infected with worms. His eyes grew red and swollen. High fevers with chills only added to excruciating pain. Sleeplessness, delirium, and choking filled his days. His horrid sickness emaciated his body.[1]

Job moved outside the city walls to the town's garbage dump, the home for the city's outcasts. He sat alone, isolated and mourning his terrible, lonely fate.

Finally, his marriage tore asunder. After ten funerals and a husband hopelessly ill, Mrs. Job had had enough. Her recommendation to her husband: "Are you still holding on to your integrity? Curse God and die!" (Job 2:9).

What makes this story so bewildering is the undeserved nature of his suffering.

Job was innocent. There was no connection between his sin and the amount of pain he experienced. This seems terribly unfair.

Where is the love and goodness of God who would do this to faithful Job?

GETTING OUT OF THE PAIN

How might you have responded to such cataclysmic loss? How might you have grieved if you were Job?

Grieving differs from family to family, from culture to culture. What our families of origin consider acceptable ways of expressing emotions related to loss shape us. Our culture also plays a role for us—be it Native American, Latino, Chinese, Arab, African American, Jewish, Eastern European, or Caucasian. At one extreme, Americans of British ancestry tend to value a "no muss, no fuss" rationale of experiencing loss. Funerals, for example, are practical and pragmatic. As one sister said, explaining why she had not attended the funeral of her twin sister, "What would have been the point of spending money on the airfare to get there? She was already dead."

On the other extreme is where time stops forever. In places like Italy and Greece, women traditionally have worn black the rest of their lives after their husband's death. In Italian-American funerals (my background) family members might bang on the coffin with their fists, crying out the dead person's name or even jumping into the grave as the coffin is lowered into the ground.

Queen Victoria of England lost her husband, Albert, when she was forty-two. Obsessed that nothing would change, she continued to make Albert the center of her life. For years she slept with his nightshirt in her arms. She made his room a "sacred room" to be kept exactly as it had been when he was alive. Every day for the rest of her long life, she had the linens changed, his clothes laid out fresh, and water prepared for his shaving. On every bed on which Queen Victoria slept, she attached a photograph of Albert as he lay dead.[2]

In our culture, addiction has become the most common way to deal with pain. We watch television incessantly. We keep busy, running from one activity to another. We work seventy hours a week, indulge in pornography, overeat, drink, take pills—anything to help us avoid the pain. Some of us demand that someone or something (a marriage, sexual partner, an ideal family, children, an achievement, a career, or a church) take our loneliness away.

Sadly, the result of denying and minimizing our wounds over many years is that we become less and less human, empty Christian shells with painted smiley faces. For some, a dull, low-level depression descends upon us, making us nearly unresponsive to all reality.

Much of contemporary Christian culture has added to this inhuman and unbiblical avoidance of pain and loss. We feel guilty for not obeying Scripture's commands to "rejoice in the Lord always" (Philippians 4:4) and to "come before him with joyful songs" (Psalm 100:2).

Deep down, many of us feel ashamed like Joe, a visitor to New Life who said to me recently: "Feeling sad or depressed or anxious about the future has got to be due to my unbelief. This is not God. It has to be related to my sins. I just figured it was better I stay away from church and Christians for a while until I get over it."

DROPPING OUR DEFENSIVE SHIELDS

Hilda, a young Jewish student, worked part time at a New York university. When a fellow student, a Christian, died of cancer, she attended the funeral. As the service began, the family announced that this would not be a time for mourning but a celebration. They remembered and thanked God for the gift of their daughter who died. They sang songs of praise. They quoted Scripture about God working all things together for good to those who love him (see Romans 8:28). In disbelief, Hilda sat through the service, wondering, *Are these people for real? Do they have any emotions at all?*

By the time she returned to work the next day, she was angry, livid that the tragic loss of her friend had been treated so glibly, Finally, she exploded at lunch to another Christian acquaintance at her job who also attended the funeral, "Don't you people cry or mourn? I don't get it. Are you people human beings at all?!"

Certainly we are not to cry or mourn like those who are without hope in Christ. But we do cry and grieve. The wise teacher of Ecclesiastes teaches us: "There is a time for everything, and a season for every activity under heaven . . . a time to weep and a time to laugh, a time to mourn and a time to dance" (Ecclesiastes 3:1, 4). Jesus himself wept, both at the grave of Lazarus and for his people in Jerusalem (see John 11:35 and Luke 19:41).

Jane, a member of our small group this past year, was becoming increasingly aware of how much she had lost in her childhood, teen, and young adult years. Our group was in the third week of exploring how both our families and ethnic histories have impacted our present lives. Jane looked terrified. For the first time in her life, she was turning toward her losses, not avoiding them.

One week, after our group, I asked her how she was doing. She responded, with her head down, in a whisper, "Pete, I keep thinking that if I continue going down this road of truly grieving my losses, I might die."

Turning toward our pain is counterintuitive. But in fact, the heart of Christianity is that the way to life is through death, the pathway to resurrection is through crucifixion. Of course, it preaches easier than it lives.

Gerald Sittser, in his book *A Grace Disguised*, reflects on the loss of his mother, wife, and young daughter from a horrific car accident. He chose not to run from his loss but to walk directly into the darkness, letting the experience of that overwhelming tragedy transform his life.

He learned that the quickest way to reach the sun and the light of day is not to run west chasing after it, but to head east into the darkness until you finally reach the sunrise.[3]

When we are children, creating a defensive wall to shield us from pain can serve as one of God's great gifts to us. If someone suffers emotional or sexual abuse as a young child, for example, denial of the assault on his or her exposed humanity serves as a healthy survival mechanism. Blocking out the pain enables him or her to endure such painful circumstances. It is healthy to not fully experience painful realities when we are that young so that we survive emotionally.

The transition into adulthood, however, requires that we mature through our "defense mechanisms" of denial in favor of honestly looking at what is true—at reality. Jesus himself said, "You will know the truth, and the truth will set you free" (John 8:32).

Unconsciously, however, we carry many defensive maneuvers into adulthood to protect ourselves from pain. And in adulthood, they block us from growing up spiritually and emotionally.

The following are a few common defenses:[4]

- *denial* (or selective forgetting)—We refuse to acknowledge some painful aspect of reality externally or internally. For example: "I feel just fine. It didn't bother me a bit that my boss belittled me . . . and that I got fired. I'm not worried in the least."
- *minimizing*—We admit something is wrong, but in such a way that it appears less serious than it actually is: "My son is doing okay with God. He's just drinking once in a while," when in reality he is drinking heavily and rarely sleeping at home.
- *blaming others*—We deny responsibility for our behavior and project it "out there" upon another: "The reason my brother is sick in the hospital is because the doctors messed up his medications!"
- *blaming yourself*—We inwardly take on the fault: "It's my fault Mom doesn't take care of me and drinks all the time. It's because I'm not worth it."

- *rationalizing*—We offer excuses, justifications, alibis to provide an inaccurate explanation of what is going on: "Did you know that John has a genetic disposition toward rage that runs in his family? That's why the meetings aren't helping him."
- *intellectualizing*—We give analysis, theories, and generalities to avoid personal awareness and difficult feelings: "My situation is not that bad compared to how others are suffering in the world. What do I have to cry about?"
- *distracting*—We change the subject or engage in humor to avoid threatening topics: "Why are you so focused on the negative? Look at the great time we had as a family last Christmas."
- *becoming hostile*—We get angry or irritable when reference is made to certain subjects: "Don't talk about Joe. He's dead. It's not going to bring him back."

BIBLICAL GRIEVING IN JOB: GOD'S PATH TO NEW BEGINNINGS

Job models brilliantly for us how we are to grieve in the family of Jesus, regardless of our family, temperament, culture, or gender. He models for us five different phases of biblical grieving so central to our following of Jesus. It is a new, radical way for most of us.

1. Pay Attention

In the church we have little theology for anger, sadness, waiting, and depression. "How are you?" we are asked after a loss or disappointment in our lives. "Couldn't be better!" we exclaim confidently without thinking. "God's working all things for good. I just can't see it all yet!"

Job, on the other hand, screamed out in his pain, holding nothing back. He cursed the day of his birth: "May the day of my birth perish, and the night it was said, 'A boy is born!' That day—may it turn to darkness. . . . If only my anguish could be weighed and all my misery be placed on the scales! It would surely outweigh the sand of the seas. . . . The arrows of the Almighty are in me, my spirit drinks in their poison; God's terrors are marshaled against me" (Job 3:3–4; 6:2–4).

He shouted at God. He prayed wild prayers. He told God exactly what he was feeling. For thirty-five chapters we read how he struggled with God. He doubted. He wept. He wondered where God is and why all this has happened to him. He did not avoid the horror of his predicament but confronted it directly.

Two-thirds of the psalms are laments, complaints to God. God grieves in Genesis for having created humanity (see Genesis 6:6). David wrote poetry after the death of Saul and his best friend, Jonathan, commanding his army to sing a lament to God (see 2 Samuel 1:17–27). Jeremiah wrote an entire Old Testament book entitled Lamentations. Ezekiel lamented. Daniel grieved. Jesus wept over Lazarus and cried out in grief over Jerusalem (see John 11:35 and Luke 13:34).

As men and women made in God's image, what has happened to us?

The psalms have been called a school of prayer. One biblical scholar wrote, in an article entitled "God Damn God: A Reflection on Expressing Anger in Prayer": "The Psalms have often been called a school of prayer. If this is true, then it must be said that Christians, in recent years at least, have been quite selective in their approach to the curriculum. A significant number of psalms have been deemed unacceptable for use in worship. These are the cursing or imprecatory psalms."[5]

We are uncomfortable with such rare, confusing bluntness.

When I became a Christian, I was taught that anger was a sin. Wanting to be like Jesus, I stuffed all feelings of irritation, annoyance, resentment, and hatred. They were sins, right?

Yes and no.

When we do not process before God the very feelings that make us human, such as fear or sadness or anger, we leak.[6] Our churches are filled with "leaking" Christians who have not treated their emotions as a discipleship issue. Grieving is not possible without paying attention to our anger and sadness. Most people who fill churches are "nice" and "respectable." Few explode in anger—at least in public. The majority, like me, stuff these "difficult feelings," trusting that God will honor our noble efforts. The result is that we leak through in soft ways such as passive-aggressive behavior (e.g., showing up late), sarcastic remarks, a nasty tone of voice, and the giving of the "silent treatment."

The following story from the movie *Ordinary People* (based on the novel by Judith Guest) illustrates the destructive consequences of refusing to wrestle with God in our sadness and anger. In the movie, Calvin and Beth Hutton are living the American dream in an affluent, Chicago suburb. Their beautiful home, along with their marriage, appears perfect. Calvin is a lawyer. Beth is a homemaker. Everything is in place.

The beauty of their stability begins to crumble when their oldest teenage son, Buck, drowns tragically in a boating accident. His younger brother, Conrad, who was with him when he drowned, feels responsible for his brother's death. Soon afterward, he attempts suicide and spends four months in a psychiatric hospital.

The movie opens a few months later with Conrad beginning his senior year in high school. He is depressed and trying to "control" himself. Neither Conrad nor his parents are able to speak openly of their profound loss and grief.

Conrad begins to see a psychiatrist twice a week and explores his interior. He slowly allows himself to be honest with his pain, his shame, his guilt about his brother's death. He admits the coldness he feels from his mother (Buck was her favorite son) and his preoccupation with "looking good" to others.

Calvin, his father, feels the increasing tension as Conrad begins to break invisible family rules and express himself. He finally attempts to speak honestly with his wife, Beth. "Wouldn't it be easier if we talked about it—in the open?" he asks.

Beth defends herself. "What are we going to talk about, for God's sake? I've already had enough changes in my life. Let's hold on to what we've got. I don't want to change. . . . I don't want any surprises. . . . I want to hold on to what I've got. We'll solve our problems in the privacy of our own home."

It is too late, however. Even a three-week vacation "away from it all" does not stop the crumbling of the false shell that has masked the true reality of their family underneath.

Calvin finally begins speaking the truth to Beth: "We were going to our son's funeral and you were worrying about what I was wearing on my feet!"

Beth cannot, and will not, respond.

The movie finally ends with Calvin sitting alone in the early morning darkness at the dining room table, crying.

Beth enters and asks what's wrong.

He quietly answers, "You are beautiful and you are unpredictable. But you're so cautious. . . ."

Calvin pauses and takes a deep breath. "It would be all right if there hadn't been any mess. But you can't handle mess. You need everything neat and easy. I don't know. . . . Maybe you can't love anybody. So much Buck. When Buck died—it was as if you buried all your love with him and I don't understand that. . . . Maybe it wasn't even Buck. . . . Maybe it was just you. But whatever it was I don't know who you are, what we've been playing at. . . . So I was crying . . . because I don't know if I love you anymore, and I don't know what I am going to do without that."

Beth slowly turns away, walks up the stairs, and goes to their bedroom.

She breaks down briefly. Then she regains her composure as she packs her bags and leaves quietly in a taxi. The marriage ends.

Beth's refusal to pay attention to her pain and loss deaden her ability to love as well. Something has died within her.

Job's misery lasted for several months, perhaps several years. We do not know. What we do know is that he paid attention to both God and himself, choosing to enter the confusion of his personal "dark night of the soul" rather than to medicate himself. We enjoy the fruits of his decision to this day.

2. Wait in the Confusing In-Between

I hate waiting for subways, buses, airplanes, and people. Like most New Yorkers, I struggle not to finish other people's sentences. I talk too fast.

My greatest challenge in following Jesus Christ for over thirty years has been waiting on God when things are confusing. I prefer control. I understand why Abraham, after waiting eleven years for God's promise of a son to come true, took matters in his own hands and had a baby the "natural way." Birthing Ishmaels is common in both our churches and personal lives. "Be still before the LORD and wait patiently for him" (Psalm 37:7) remains one of the most radical commands of our day. It requires enormous humility.

Job waited for a long time when the people closest to him quit. They did not have a big enough God or theology to walk through phase two of grieving—waiting in the confusing in-between. Job spent much time battling with his three religious friends—Eliphaz, Zophar, and Bildad—who were convinced Job was suffering because of his sin.

"That is the way God works," they argued time and time again. "You reap what you sow, Job, and you must have done some bad things. You need to repent so God can bless you once again. You are suffering due to your sin. Trouble comes to sinners."

Job's three friends represent "classic religion" or "legalism." It goes something like this: "The reason you are not healed is you don't pray enough, fast enough, read the Bible enough. You are suffering more than most because you have sinned more."

The problem with Job is that it wasn't true. He was an innocent sufferer. His friends had no room for the "confusing in-between," no room for mystery. Like many Christians today, they overestimated their grasp of truth. They played God and stood in God's shoes. Job had two fights going on: one with God and the other with his friends who kept quoting Scripture to him. They tried to fix Job and defend God, and in their attempt to explain what God was doing (which they did not understand), they tortured Job, who was already in great pain.

Do you know what it is like to feel worse after talking with some people who were trying to make you feel better?

The confusing in-between resists all earthly categories and quick solutions. It runs contrary to our Western culture that pervades our spirituality. It is for this reason we have such an aversion to the limits God places around us.

3. Embrace the Gift of Limits

I have wondered if the greatest loss we must grieve is our limits. It drives us to humility before God and others like little else. Great as Job was, he was not God. He, too, had to embrace his limits.

Consider the following list of your limits:

- your physical body—Your body is dying and will return to dust one day. You must sleep, eat, and drink in order to live. All the plastic surgeons in the world, ultimately, cannot stop your aging process. We will finish our lives with unfinished goals and dreams.
- your family of origin—Your family, ethnicity, country of birth, culture all gave you a gift and limits. Whether you had two parents, one parent, or were adopted, all of us enter adulthood with limits given to us by our families.
- your marital status—Both marriage and singleness are limits given by God. If you have children, the number and kind of children is a limit.
- your intellectual capacity—None of us is brilliant in literature, mathematics, engineering, carpentry, physics, and music at the same time.
- your talents and gifts—Jesus has all the gifts. You may have ten. I may have three. Only Jesus has them all.
- your material wealth—Even if you are a millionaire, you are limited in your resources. Our level of prosperity limits us.
- your raw material—God has given you a certain personality, temperament, "unique self." I am a high feeler and an extrovert. That is both a gift and limit. It is great for writing and speaking and creating. It limits me in leading a large staff and church.
- your time—You have only one life to live. You can't do it all. I would like to try living in Asia, Europe, Africa, and a rural area in the United States. I would like to try a few different professions. I can't. My time is running out.
- your work and relationship realities—Our work remains

"thorns and thistles" (Genesis 3:18). It is hard. We never totally finish. There is always a grief in never having complete fulfillment. Relationships will not be perfect until heaven. Who wouldn't like a perfect, loving church where everyone has the time, energy, and maturity to love everyone else perfectly! We must grieve that limit also or we will demand from them something they cannot give.

- your spiritual understanding—"The secret things belong to the LORD our God" (Deuteronomy 29:29). God has revealed himself to us in his Son, Scripture, creation, and other ways, but so much of who he is remains incomprehensible.

John the Baptist models wonderfully for us what it means to embrace our limits. Crowds that formerly followed John for baptism switched their allegiances once Jesus began his ministry. They began leaving John to follow Jesus. Some of John's followers were upset about this dramatic turn of events. They complained to him, "Everyone is going to him" (John 3:26).

John understood limits and replied, "A man can receive only what is given him from heaven" (John 3:27). He was able to say, "I accept my limits, my humanity, my declining popularity. He must increase. I must decrease" (see John 3:30).

In contrast, many of us are like a baby. A baby screams for his mother to feed and take care of him. He is the center of the universe, with others existing to care for his needs. He suffers from grandiosity, arrogance, childishness. Growing up will require learning he is not the center of the universe. The universe does not exist to meet his every need.

That is a painful lesson for all of us to learn. Our egos tend to be so inflated that we act as if we were God. Often we have larger fantasies and wishes for ourselves than our real lives can support. As a result, we work frantically trying to do more than God intended. We burn out thinking we can do more than we can. We get stressed and blame others. We run around frantically, convinced that the world—whether it be our churches, friends, businesses, or children—will stop if we stop.

Others of us get depressed because our desires are so high and unachievable that it seems useless to do anything at all.[7]

Getting off our thrones and joining the rest of humanity is a must for growing up. A part of us hates limits. We won't accept them. This is part of the reason why grieving loss biblically is such an indispensable part of spiritual maturity. It humbles us like little else.

In fact, one of the great tasks of parenting and leadership is to help others accept their limits. This applies to the home, workplace, community, or church.

4. Climb the Ladder of Humility

Job emerged from his suffering transformed. He was a broken and changed man.

After his great loss and long time of waiting, God spoke to Job out of the storm of his life. For the first time, God referred to him four times as "my servant," suggesting a new level of intimacy and closeness with Job (see Job 42). Job had the opportunity to take revenge on his three religious friends who tortured him with their proud, insensitive counsel. Instead he prayed and blessed them (see Job 42:7–9). Throughout the process of waiting, Job made a choice. It was a choice to "climb the ladder of humility," something Jesus described as an indispensable quality for maturing in him (Matthew 5:3–10; Luke 14:7–11; 18:9–14).

St. Benedict, in the sixth century, developed a twelve-step ladder for growing in the grace of humility. His goal was perfect love and transformation of our entire personalities. I don't know too many Christians today seeking to climb this ladder. (Like anything else, this, too, can be misused. But I believe it is a powerful, time-tested tool when used with the other elements of emotional health.)

On the following page is my adaptation of St. Benedict's Ladder of Humility.[8]

St. Benedict's Ladder of Humility

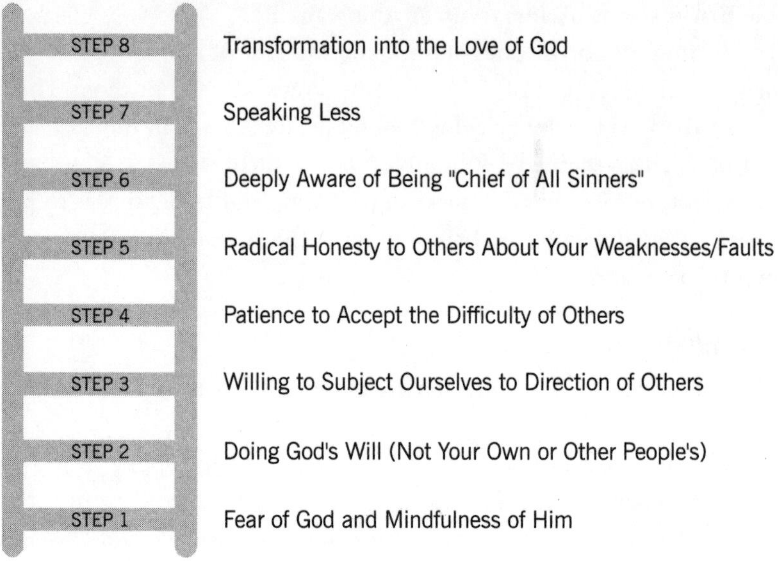

STEP 1: Fearful of God and Mindfulness of Him—We often forget the presence of God, acting as if he were not present.

STEP 2: Busy Doing God's Will (Not Our Own or Other People's) —We recognize that surrendering our self-will to God's will for our lives touches the very heart of spiritual transformation.

STEP 3: Willing to Subject Ourselves to Direction of Others—We are free to give up our arrogance and all-powerfulness and are open to accepting God's will as it comes through others. This may be a manager at work, or directions from a friend. And we do it without grumbling or an attitude.

STEP 4: Patient to Accept the Difficulties of Others—Life with others, especially when living in community, is full of aggravations. This requires we give others a chance to figure out their weakness their own way in their own time.

STEP 5: Radical Honesty to Others About Our Weaknesses/Faults —We quit pretending to be something we are not. We admit our weaknesses and limitations to a friend, spouse, parent, or someone else who cares about our development.

STEP 6: Deeply Aware of Being Chief of All Sinners—We see ourselves as potentially weaker and more sinful than anyone around us. We are the chief of all sinners. This is not self-hate or an invitation to abuse, but is meant to make us kind and gentle.

STEP 7: Purposeful to Speak Less (with More Restraint)—This is near the top of the ladder, because it is seen as the outcome of a life that seeks God and is filled with wisdom. As the Rule of St. Benedict states: "The wise are known for their few words."

STEP 8: Transformed into the Love of God—Here, there is no haughtiness, no sarcasm, no put downs, no airs of importance. We are able to embrace our limits and those of others. We are fully aware of how fragile we are and are under no illusions. We are at home with ourselves and content to rely on the mercy of God. Everything is a gift.

LET THE OLD BIRTH THE NEW

Good grieving is not just letting go, but also letting it bless us. Job did just that. The old life for Job was truly over. That door remained closed. That is the great grief about our losses. There is finality. We can't get it back. Yet when we follow Job's path and . . .

1. Pay Attention
2. Wait in the Confusing In-Between
3. Embrace the Gift of Limits
4. Climb the Ladder of Humility
5. Let the Old Birth the New . . . *in his time*

. . . we will be blessed. That is the lesson of Job. As he followed the difficult path of allowing his losses to enlarge his soul for God, God blessed him superabundantly. Not only was he spiritually transformed but "the LORD made him prosperous again and gave him twice as much as he had before. . . The LORD blessed the latter part of Job's life more than the first." His wealth was doubled. God gave him ten children once again and he lived till a ripe old age (see Job 42:10–17).

This account is meant to encourage us to trust the living God with the many mini-deaths that we experience in our lives. The central message of Christ is that suffering and death bring resurrection and transformation. Jesus himself said, "I tell you the truth, unless a kernel of wheat falls to the ground and dies, it remains only a single seed. But if it dies, it produces many seeds" (John 12:24).

But remember, resurrection only comes out of death—real death. Our losses are real.

And so is our God, the living God.

A NEW RELATIONSHIP WITH GOD

There are many rich fruits that blossom in our lives as a result of embracing our losses. The greatest, however, concerns our relationship to God. We move from a "Give me, give me, and give me" prayer life to an intimate, loving prayer life characterized by loving union with God.[9] When we grieve God's way, we are changed forever.

In the next chapter, we will examine more closely two disciplines in the history of God's people—the Daily Office and the Sabbath—and why they are so essential to a more mature prayer life as well an emotionally healthy spirituality.

Lord Jesus, when I think about my losses, it can feel that I have no skin to protect me. I feel raw, scraped to the bone. I don't know why you have allowed such pain. Looking at Job helps, but I must admit that I struggle to see something "new being birthed out of the old." Lord, grant me the courage to feel, to pay attention, and then to wait on you. You know that everything in me resists limits, humility, and the cross. So I invite you, Father, Son, and Holy Spirit, to make your home in me as you describe in John 14:23, to freely roam and fill every crevice of my life. And may the prayer of Job, finally, be mine: "My ears had heard of you but now my eyes have seen you." In Jesus' name, amen.

CHAPTER EIGHT

DISCOVER THE RHYTHMS OF THE DAILY OFFICE AND SABBATH

Stopping to Breathe the Air of Eternity

We live in a blizzard. And few of us have a rope.

In his book *A Hidden Wholeness* Parker Palmer relates a story about farmers in the Midwest who would prepare for blizzards by tying a rope from the back door of their house out to the barn as a guide to ensure they could return safely home. These blizzards came quickly and fiercely and were highly dangerous. When their full force was blowing, a farmer could not see the end of his or her hand. Many froze to death in those blizzards, disoriented by their inability to see. They wandered in circles, lost sometimes in their own backyards. If they lost their grip on the rope, it became impossible for them to find their way home. Some froze within feet of their own front door, never realizing how close they were to safety.

To this day, in parts of Canada and the Great Plains, meteorologists counsel people that, to avoid getting lost in the blinding snow when they venture outside, they tie one end of a long rope to their house and grasp the other end firmly.[1]

Many of us have lost our way, spiritually, in the whiteout of the blizzard swirling around us. Blizzards begin when we say yes to too many things. Between demands from work and family, our lives fall somewhere between *full* and *overflowing*. We multitask, so much so that we are unaware we are doing three things at once. We admire people who are able to accomplish so much in so little time. They are our role models.

At the same time many of us are overscheduled, tense, addicted to hurry, frantic, preoccupied, fatigued, and starved for time. Cramming as much as possible into our Blackberries and Palm Pilots, day planners and to-do lists, we battle life to make the best use of every spare minute we have.

Yet not much changes. Our overproductivity becomes counterproductive. We end our days exhausted from work and raising children. And then our "free time" on weekends becomes filled with more demands in an already-overburdened life.

We listen to sermons and read books about slowing down and creating margin in our lives.[2] We read about the need to rest and recharge our batteries. Our workplaces offer seminars on increased productivity through replenishing ourselves.

But we can't stop. And if we aren't busy, we feel guilty that we waste time and are not productive.

We go through the motions of doing so many things as if there is no alternative way of spending our days. It is like being addicted—only it is not to drugs or alcohol but to tasks, to work, to doing. Any sense of rhythm in our daily, weekly, and yearly lives has been swallowed up in the blizzard of our lives.

Add to this the storms and trials of life that blow into our lives unexpectedly and catch us off guard, and we wonder why so many of us are disoriented and confused.

We need a rope to lead us home.

God *is* offering us a rope to keep us from getting lost. This rope consistently leads us back home to him, to a place that is centered and rooted. This rope can be found in two ancient disciplines going back thousands of years—the Daily Office and Sabbath. When placed inside present-day Christianity, the Daily Office and Sabbath are ground-breaking, countercultural acts against Western culture. They are powerful declarations about God, ourselves, our relationships, our beliefs, and our values.

Stopping for the Daily Office and Sabbath is not meant to add another to-do to our already-busy schedules. It is the resetting of our entire lives toward a new destination—God. It is an entirely new way of being in the world.

The Daily Office and Sabbath are ropes that lead us back to God in the blizzards of life. They are anchors for living in the hurricane of demands. When done as a "want to" rather than a "have to," they offer us a rhythm for our lives that binds us to the living God.

They are nothing short of revolutionary disciplines for Christians today.

THE INADEQUACY OF OUR PRESENT ROPES

Today we teach young Christians eager to develop their relationship with God to have devotions or a quiet time. Normally this consists of ten to thirty minutes a day spent reading the Bible, praying, and perhaps reading something from a devotional book. Along with church on Sundays and perhaps involvement in a small group, we hope this will enable them to withstand the blizzard swirling around them.

It won't.

Within a couple of hours after being with God in the morning, I easily forgot God was active in my everyday affairs. By lunch I was grumpy and short with people. By late afternoon God's presence had disappeared from my consciousness. By the time dinner was over, he felt a long way off. After observing my behavior for a couple of hours, my wife and children were always wondering, "What happened to Dad's Christianity?" And by nine o'clock at night, I was asking myself the same question!

I wanted to pay attention to God all through the day. I longed to be carried in his presence like Brother Lawrence wrote about in *Practicing the Presence of God*. The emotional health integration Geri and I had worked on for years had dramatically changed people's lives. But something continued to elude us. We knew the answer related to a further slowing down the pace of people's lives and their balancing of activity and contemplation. Yes, embracing our limits was helpful, but something was still missing.

There are many great spiritual disciplines—the prayer of examen, retreats, spiritual direction, service, fellowship in small groups, worship, giving, Bible study, devotional reading, centering prayer, fasting, Scripture memorization, *lectio divina*, confession, journaling, intercession, to name a few.[3] They are each wonderful tools and gifts for us in our following of Jesus. Many are essential threads in a strong rope to keep us centered and lead us home in the midst of blizzards.

The Daily Office and the Sabbath, however, offer us a rhythm so powerful that they anchor us from whatever catastrophic blizzard that may be blowing in our lives so we can feel the rope (that is, God himself) and make our way home.

STOPPING TO SURRENDER

At the heart of the Daily Office and the Sabbath is stopping to surrender to God in trust. Failure to do so is the very essence of the sin in the Garden of Eden. Adam and Eve legitimately worked and enjoyed their achievements in the garden. They were to embrace their limits, however, and not eat from the tree of the knowledge of good and evil. They were not to try to see and know that which belongs to the almighty God. God was teaching them that, "after the full flowering of their achievements and activities, they [were] invited, not to be active, not to accomplish, but to surrender in trust. . . . Action, then passivity; striving, then letting go, doing all one can do and then being carried . . . only in this rhythm is the spirit realized."[4]

As theologian Robert Barron argued, at the heart of original sin is the refusal to accept God's rhythm for us.[5] The essence of being in God's image is our ability, like God, to stop. We imitate God by stopping our work and resting. If we can stop for one day a week, or for mini-Sabbaths each day (the Daily Office), we touch something deep within us as image bearers of God. Our human brain, our bodies, our spirits, and our emotions become wired by God for the rhythm of work and rest in him.[6]

The Daily Office and Sabbath serve as ropes so we might live in a rhythmic and joyful way even in the midst of blizzards.

THE DISCOVERY OF AN ANCIENT TREASURE: THE DAILY OFFICE

The term *Daily Office* (also called *fixed-hour prayer*, *Divine Office*, or *liturgy of the hours*) differs from what we label today as *quiet time* or *devotions*. When I listen carefully to most people describe their devotional life, the emphasis tends to be on "getting filled up for the day" or "interceding for the needs around me." The root of the Daily Office is not so much a turning to God to get something but to be *with* Someone.

The word *Office* comes from the Latin word *opus*, or "work." For the early church, the Daily Office was always the "work of God." Nothing was to interfere with that priority. It was "an act of offering . . . by the creature to the Creator . . . prayers of praise offered as a sacrifice of thanksgiving and faith to God and as sweet-smelling incense . . . before the throne of God."[7]

I first observed and experienced the Daily Office during a one-week visit with Trappist monks in Massachusetts. The basic structure of Trappist life includes four elements—prayer, work, study, and rest. Yet it was their intentional arranging of their lives around the prayers of the Daily Office that moved me. This was their means to remain aware of God's presence while they worked and to enable them to maintain healthy balance in their lives.

During my time with the monks, we met seven times a day, remembering God through reading and singing the Scriptures, especially the psalms, and prayer. Our daily schedule looked like this:

Vigils: 3:45 AM (middle of the night)
Lauds: 6:00 AM (predawn)
Prime: 6:25 AM ("First" hour—in their case it was Mass)
Sext: 12:15 PM ("Sixth" hour)
None: 2:00 PM ("Ninth" hour)
Vespers 5:40 PM ("Evening" hour)

Compline: 7:40 PM (before bed)

We chanted so many psalms (they sing all one hundred and fifty each week), read so much Scripture, and spent so much time in silence that by day three of my first week I felt like I had been transported into another world. I cannot imagine what that would do to a person's spiritual life if they engaged in that kind of spiritual discipline 365 days a year, year after year, decade after decade.

I did not join the monks in their six hours of manual work, but spent that time taking naps! I was too physically exhausted. (My body was not accustomed to getting up at 3:15 AM.) Yet I was sure of one thing: this rhythm of pausing for the Daily Office offered a key to unlocking the secret of paying attention to God and being carried in his presence throughout the day unlike anything I had experienced in almost thirty years of following Christ.

What surprised me most in conversations with them was how much we had in common in our love for Christ and our desire to be transformed by that love and into that love. They, too, struggled with the balance of "Mary" and "Martha," activity and contemplation.

This experience with the Trappists launched me on a journey over the next two years to visit a variety of Roman Catholic, Protestant, and Orthodox monastic communities to learn more. From Taizé, France, to the Northumbrian community in England to the monks of New Skete in upstate New York, Geri and I participated in all kinds of variations of the Daily Office. And I read church history—a lot of it—trying to understand how this might apply to schoolteachers, police officers, lawyers, social workers, contractors, students, financial advisors, and stay-at-home moms seeking to follow Jesus in a place like New York City.

More importantly, I was trying to figure out how it might apply to me—a husband and father of four daughters with a full-time job as a pastor of a very active church with enormous demands for my time. How might I integrate this in the midst of soccer games, teachers meetings, tuition decisions, parenting issues, neighboring relationships, and faucet leaks?

David practiced set times of prayer seven times a day (see Psalm

119:164). Daniel prayed three times a day (see Daniel 6:10). Devout Jews in Jesus' time prayed two to three times a day. Jesus himself probably followed the Jewish custom of praying at set times during the day. After Jesus' resurrection, his disciples continued to pray at certain hours of the day (see Acts 3:1 and 10:9ff).

About A.D. 525, a good man named Benedict structured these prayer times around eight Daily Offices, including one in the middle of the night for monks. The Rule of St. Benedict became one of the most powerful documents in shaping Western civilization. At one point in his Rule, Benedict wrote: "On hearing the signal for an hour of the divine office, the monk will immediately set aside what he has in hand and go with utmost speed. . . . Indeed, nothing is to be preferred to the Work of God [that is, the Daily Office]."[8]

All these people realized that the stopping for the Daily Office to be with God is the key to creating a continual and easy familiarity with God's presence the rest of the day. It is the rhythm of stopping that makes the "practice of the presence of God," to use Brother Lawrence's phrase, a real possibility.

I know it does for me. The great power in setting apart small units of time for morning, midday, and evening prayer infuses into the rest of my day's activities a deep sense of the sacred, of God. All the time is his. The Daily Office, practiced consistently, actually eliminates any division of the sacred and the secular in our lives.

THE CENTRAL ELEMENTS OF THE DAILY OFFICE

God has built us each differently. What works for one person will not for another. Geri and I approach our Daily Offices very differently. I prefer more structure, enjoy written prayers, pray the psalms often, and love the rhythm of four Offices per day.

Geri utilizes a variety of tools, books, methods to approach her Daily Office each day. She will skip an Office without any guilt whatsoever. She aims at three Offices a day and enjoys great flexibility to what she does in her time with God. For example, it is not uncommon for Geri to go outside and breathe in the presence of God in creation.

You choose the length of time for your Offices. The key, remember, is regular remembrance of God, not length. Your pausing to be with God can last anywhere from two minutes to twenty minutes to forty-five minutes. It is up to you.

You also choose the content of your Offices. A number of possible resources are available that you may want to utilize—*The Divine Hours* by Phyllis Tickle, *Celtic Daily Prayer* by the Northumbria Community, and *A Guide to Prayer for All Who Seek God* by Norman Shawchuck and Rueben P. Job are three excellent examples.[9] Many of us also utilize the daily examen of St. Ignatius for compline (see appendix A). *Compline* refers to the final office/prayer time at the completion of the day before going to sleep.

Yet four elements, I believe, need to be found in any Office, regardless of what approach you ultimately choose. The Office can be done together or alone.

1. Stopping

This is the essence of a Daily Office. What is more important than the number of offices each day is that our time with God be unhurried so that what we read or pray has time to sink deeply into our spirits. We stop our activity and pause to be with the living God. Central to the challenge of stopping at midday, for example, is to trust that God is on the throne. He rules. I don't. At each Office I give up control and trust God to run his world without me.

2. Centering

Scripture commands us: "Be still before the LORD and wait patiently for him" (Psalm 37:7) and "Be still, and know that I am God" (Psalm 46:10). We move into God's presence and rest there. That alone is no small feat. For this reason I often spend five minutes centering down so I can let go of my tensions, distractions, and sensations and begin resting in the love of God. I follow James Finley's guidelines for these times:[10]

- Be attentive and open
- Sit still
- Sit straight

- Breathe slowly, deeply, and naturally
- Close your eyes or lower them to the ground

When you find your mind wandering, let your breathing bring you back. As you breathe in, ask God to fill you with the Holy Spirit. As you breathe out, exhale all that is sinful, false, and not of him.

A second tool I use when my mind wanders is to pray the Jesus Prayer: "Lord Jesus Christ, Son of God, have mercy on me, a sinner." If nothing else happens during a Daily Office, it is a call to mindfulness, an invitation to pay attention to what our short, earthly lives are all about.

3. Silence

Dallas Willard has called *silence* and *solitude* the two most radical disciplines of the Christian life. Solitude is the practice of being absent from people and things to attend to God. Silence is the practice of quieting every inner and outer voice to attend to God. Henri Nouwen said that "without solitude it is almost impossible to live a spiritual life."[11]

These are probably the most challenging and least practiced disciplines among Christians today. We live in a world of noise and distractions. Most of us fear silence. Studies say that the average group can only bear fifteen seconds of silence. Most of our church services confirm this.

When God appeared to Elijah after his suicidal depression and flight from Jezebel, he told him to stand and wait for the presence of the Lord to pass by. God did not appear in ways he had in the past. God was not in the wind (as with Job), an earthquake (as at Mount Sinai with the giving of the Ten Commandments), or fire (as in the burning bush with Moses). God finally revealed himself to Elijah in "a sound of sheer whisper" (see 1 Kings 19:12). The translation of God coming in "a still small voice"(KJV) does not capture the original Hebrew but what could the translators do? How do you hear silence!?

The silence after the chaos, for Elijah and for us, is full of the presence of God. God did speak to Elijah out of the silence, and he speaks also to us. While it is not the objective of the Office, it is a natural result.

4. Scripture

The psalms are the foundation of almost any Daily Office book you will find available today. They have served as the prayer book of the church through the centuries. Jesus quoted psalms more than any other book except Isaiah. The prayers of the Psalter cover the entire gamut of our life experience—from anger to rage to trust to praise. A good Daily Office guide will also lead you to Old and New Testament readings that both reflect the church calendar year and a balanced diet of spiritual food. I often conclude each Daily Office by slowly and thoughtfully praying the Lord's Prayer.

There are many other rich spiritual practices you can integrate into your Daily Office—*lectio divina* (meditation on Scripture), centering prayer, singing along with a worship CD, or reading through the Bible in a year, readings from devotional classics, to name a few.[12]

A good rule to follow when dealing with tools and techniques is this: If it helps, do it. If it does not help you, do not do it—including the Daily Office!! If reading the psalms helps you, then great. Do it. If reading the psalms has become routine and dead for you, then don't. Maybe it is time for you to meditate on one phrase, such as "You hem me in—behind and before; you have laid your hand upon me" (Psalm 139:5) and sit in silence. Be attentive in your heart to what God is doing inside of you. Learn from others. Remember: we go through seasons. And most important, let God be your guide.

The purpose of the Daily Office is to remember God and commune with him all through our days. Keep that clearly in mind as you develop structures and habits that fit you. We are constantly tempted to think God will love us more if we pray more, do the Daily Office often, and keep the Sabbath. Remember grace, which reminds us there is nothing we can do or not do that would cause God to love us any more than he does right now.

We have been experimenting with how to integrate the Daily Office into our lives within our active local church in New York City. In appendix B is a simple tool we have used to help individuals and small groups get started in pausing for the Daily Office throughout the day.[13]

A SECOND ANCIENT TREASURE: SABBATH-KEEPING

The word *Sabbath* comes from the Hebrew word that means "to cease, to stop working." It refers to doing nothing related to work for a twenty-four hour period each week. It refers to this unit of time around which we are to orient our entire lives as "holy," meaning "separate, a cut above" the other six days (see Genesis 2:2–3).[14] Sabbath provides for us now an additional rhythm for an entire reorientation of our lives around the living God. On Sabbaths we imitate God by stopping our work and resting.

Make no mistake about it: keeping the command to Sabbath is both radical and extremely difficult in our everyday lives. It cuts to the core of our spirituality, the core of our convictions, the core of our faith, the core of our lifestyles.

Our culture knows nothing of setting aside a whole day (twenty-four hours) to rest and delight in God. Like most, I always considered it an optional extra, not something absolutely essential to discipleship. But as we've discussed, living in a fallen world is much like being in a blizzard. Without the Sabbath, we easily find ourselves lost and unsure of the larger picture of God and our lives. I am convinced that nothing less than an understanding of Sabbath as a *command* from God, as well as an incredible invitation, will enable us to grab hold of this rope God offers us.

GOD'S COMMAND FOR RHYTHM IN OUR LIVES

Keeping the Sabbath in Scripture is a commandment—right next to refraining from lying, murdering, and committing adultery. Sabbath is a gift from God we are invited to receive.

Israel lived as slaves in Egypt for over four hundred years. They never had a day off. They were treated as tools of production to make pyramids. They were "doing" machines. They worked seven days a week all year long. Imagine how deeply ingrained activism and overwork must have been for them! They had never observed or experienced a rhythm of work and rest. They had neither permission nor the choice to do so. Living meant performing tasks, with one day blurring into the next.

When God called Israel out of Egypt, he affirmed they were sacred human beings made in his image. He then showed them how to live according to their God-given nature. In effect, God said, "It may feel awkward at first, but as a fish is created to live in water, I created you to live according to this design."

The longest and most specific of the Ten Commandments is the fourth. Let's take a look at all of them in comparison:

- You shall have no other gods before me.
- You shall not make for yourself an idol.
- You shall not misuse the name of the Lord your God.
- Remember the Sabbath day by keeping it holy. Six days you shall labor and do all your work, but the seventh day is a Sabbath to the Lord our God. On it you shall not do any work, neither you, nor your son or daughter, nor your manservant or maidservant, nor your animals, nor the alien within your gates. For in six days the Lord made the heavens and the earth, the sea and all that is in them, but he rested on the seventh day. Therefore the LORD blessed the Sabbath day and made it holy.
- Honor your father and your mother.
- You shall not murder.
- You shall not commit adultery.
- You shall not steal.
- You shall not give false witness.
- You shall not covet. (see Exodus 20:1–17)

God worked. We are to work. God rested. We are to rest. After completing his work of creating the heavens and earth, God rested on the seventh day. It was the climax of God's week in Genesis 1:1–2:4, and it is to be the climax of ours.

Before the Israelites entered the Promised Land, Moses proclaimed further that the very act of ceasing from work in the midst of all the surrounding nations was a sign of their liberation by God (see Deuteronomy 5:13ff). By the very act of refusing to succumb to the enormous pressure of Western culture around us, we, too, serve as a sign of a free people. We have been called out of a world trying to prove its worth and value by what it does or possesses. We are deeply loved by God for who we are, not for what we do.

The Sabbath calls us to build the doing of nothing into our schedules each week. Nothing measurable is accomplished. By the world's standards it is inefficient, unproductive, and useless. As one theologian stated, "To fail to see the value of simply being with God and 'doing nothing' is to miss the heart of Christianity."[15]

The Sabbath was always a hallmark of the Jews throughout their history. This one act, perhaps more than any other, kept them from the pressure of the powerful cultures that have sought to assimilate them. For this reason it is often said that, for thirty-five hundred years, the Sabbath has kept the Jews more than Jews have kept the Sabbath.

This is certainly not the case with Christians living in the twenty-first century.

Sabbath, when lived, is our means as the people of God to bear witness to the way we understand life, its rhythms, its gifts, its meaning, and its ultimate purpose in God. Observing the Sabbath, we affirm: "God is the center and source of our lives. He is the beginning, the middle, and the end of our existence." We trust God to provide and care for us.

Eugene Peterson points out even though Sabbath has been one of the most abused and distorted practices of the Christian life, we cannot do without it. "Sabbath is not primarily about us or how it benefits us; it is about God and how God forms us. . . . I don't see any way out of it; if we are going to live appropriately in the creation we must keep the Sabbath."[16]

THE FOUR PRINCIPLES OF BIBLICAL SABBATH

One of the great dangers of faithfully observing Sabbath is legalism. What about pastors, nurses, doctors, police officers, and others who must work on Sundays? Jesus observed Sabbath but he also healed the sick and preached sermons on that day. What might be work for you may be different for someone else. Some people will have to choose another day besides Saturday or Sunday (depending on your church tradition) if it is to be a day without work.

The key is to set a regular rhythm of keeping the Sabbath every seven days for a twenty-four-hour block of time. Traditional Jewish Sabbath begins at sundown on Friday and ends on sundown Saturday. I know many Christians who begin their Sabbath precisely at 6:00 PM or 7:00 PM on Saturday until the same time the following day. Others, like myself, choose a day of the week. The apostle Paul seemed to think one day would do as well as another (see Romans 14:1–17). What is important is to select a time period and protect it!

The following are four foundational qualities of biblical Sabbaths that have served me well in distinguishing a "day off" from a biblical Sabbath. A secular Sabbath is to replenish our energies and make us more effective the other six days. A "day off" produces positive results but is, in Eugene Peterson's words, "a bastard Sabbath."[17] I commend them to you as you develop a biblical framework for Sabbath that fits your particular life situation, temperament, calling, and personality.

1. Stop

Sabbath is first and foremost a day of "stopping." "To stop" is built into the literal meaning of the Hebrew word *Sabbath*. Yet most of us can't stop until we are finished with whatever it is we think we need to do. We need to complete our projects and term papers, answer our e-mails, return all phone messages, complete the balancing of our check books to pay our bills, finish cleaning the house. There's always one more goal to be reached before stopping.

On Sabbath I embrace my limits. God is God. He is indispensable. I am his creature. The world continues working fine when I stop.

I have hated stopping my entire life. When I was a college and seminary student, I had too much homework to stop for one twenty-four-hour period. When I taught high school English, I had too many papers to grade to stop. When I was learning Spanish in Costa Rica, I couldn't stop if I was going to learn the language. If I was going to be responsive to the needs of the people in our church and still have time to pray and study, I needed to work at least half of my Sabbath, didn't I?

We think, *Maybe I will stop when our children grow into adults and are on their own, when I have enough saved to buy our first home, when I retire and* . . . The list goes on.

We stop on Sabbaths because God is on the throne, assuring us the world will not fall apart if we cease our activities. Life on this side of heaven is an unfinished symphony. We accomplish one goal and then immediately are confronted with new opportunities and challenges. But ultimately we will die with countless unfinished projects and goals. That's okay. God is at work taking care of the universe. He manages quite well without us having to run things. When we are sleeping, he is working. So he commands us to relax, to enjoy the fact that we are not in charge of his world, that even when we die, the world will continue on nicely without us. Every Sabbath reminds us to "be still, and know that [he is] God" (Psalm 46:10) and to stop worrying about tomorrow (see Matthew 6:25–33).

The core spiritual issue in stopping revolves around trust. Will God take care of us and our concerns if we obey him by stopping to keep the Sabbath?

The story is told of a wagon train of Christians traveling on their way from St. Louis to Oregon. They observed the habit of stopping for the Sabbath during the autumn but as winter approached the group began to panic in fear they would not reach their destination before the snows began. A number of members of the group proposed they quit the practice of stopping for the Sabbath and travel seven days a week. This caused an argument in the community until it was finally decided to divide the wagon train into two groups. One group would observe the Sabbath day as before and not travel. The other would press on.

Which group arrived in Oregon first? Of course—the ones who kept the Sabbath. Both the people and their horses were so rested by their Sabbath observance they could travel much more efficiently the other six days.[18]

When I trust God and obey his commands, he provides. Jesus takes our loaves and fishes that we offer him, even though they are insufficient to feed the multitudes, and somehow miraculously and invisibly multiplies them. We can trust him enough to stop.

2. Rest

Once we stop, the Sabbath calls us to rest. God rested after his work. We are to do the same—every seventh day (see Genesis 2:1–4). What do we do to replace all we are now stopping during our Sabbath time? The answer is simple: whatever delights and replenishes you.

For example, in my case work relates to my vocation as pastor of New Life Fellowship Church, along with writing and speaking. For this reason, Saturday rather than Sunday is my Sabbath. I purposely engage in ideas and people that get my mind off even the thought of work! That includes napping, working out, going for long walks, reading a novel, watching a good movie, going out for dinner. I avoid the computer and cell phone.

For me to enjoy Sabbath rest on Saturday, however, requires I have another day of the week to do the tasks of life that consume my energy or fill me with worry. For example, planning my week, paying bills, balancing our checkbook, cleaning the house, fighting traffic and crowds to shop, doing loads of laundry are all work I need to do a different day of the week.

The following list gives you nine possibilities to consider replacing with rest. The primary one, of course, is rest from work. But you may want to also pick one or two others over the next couple of months as you develop your practice of Sabbath keeping. Consider resting from:

- work
- physical exhaustion
- hurriedness
- multitasking
- competitiveness
- worry
- decision making
- catching up on errands
- talking
- technology and machines (e.g., cell phones, TV, computers, Palm Pilots)

When we stop and rest, we respect our humanity and the image of God in us. We are not nonstop human beings. Sadly, it often takes a physical illness such as cancer, a heart attack, the flu, or a severe depression to get us to rest. We don't serve the Sabbath. The Sabbath serves us.

3. Delight

A third component to biblical Sabbath revolves around delighting in what we have been given. God, after finishing his work of creation, proclaimed that "it was very good" (Genesis 1:31). God delighted over his creation. The Hebrew phrase communicates a sense of joy, completion, wonder, and play. This is particularly radical in a culture like ours, both secular and Christian, that is "delight deficient." Because of the way pleasure and delight have been so distorted by our culture, many of us as Christians struggle with receiving joy and pleasure.

On Sabbaths we are called to enjoy and delight in creation and its gifts. We are to slow down and pay attention to our food, smelling and tasting its riches. We are to take the time to see the beauty of a tree, a leaf, a flower, the sky that has been created with great care by our God. He has given us the ability to see, hear, taste, smell, and touch, that we might feast with our senses on the miraculousness of life. We are, as William Blake wrote, "to see a world in a grain of sand and a heaven in a wild flower."[19]

I will never forget the first time I took pleasure in warm water running over my hands in a McDonald's restroom on a Sabbath. I slowly dried my hands, rubbing them together under the drier as the water dissipated. I did not run out of the restroom, drying my hands on my pants as I walked to the car. I did not skip putting soap all over my hands. I relished the present moment and tasted the Sabbath gift of simply washing my hands!

On Sabbaths God also invites us to slow down to pay attention and delight in people. In the Gospels, Jesus modeled a prayerful presence with people—whether it was a Samaritan woman, the widow at Nain, the rich young ruler, or Nicodemus. He seemed "into" the beauty of men and women crafted in God's image. This has become a spiritual discipline for me. I try, for example, to walk slowly, leaving lots of free space and time on Sabbaths so I can stop for unexpected conversations with neighbors, family, and shopkeepers. I ask God for the grace to leave the frenzied busyness around me and be a contemplative presence to those around me.

Finally, Sabbath delight invites us to healthy play. The word chosen by the Greek Fathers for the perfect, mutual indwelling of the Trinity was *perichoerisis*. It literally means "dancing around."[20] Creation and life are, in a sense, God's gift of a playground to us. Whether it be through sports, dance, games, looking at old family photographs, or visiting museums, nurturing our sense of pure fun in God also is part of Sabbath.

4. Contemplate

The final quality of a biblical Sabbath is, of course, the contemplation of God. The Sabbath is always "holy to the LORD" (Exodus 31:15). Pondering the love of God remains the central focus of our Sabbaths. Throughout Jewish and Christian history, Sabbath has included worship with God's people where we feast on his presence, the reading and study of Scripture, and silence. For this reason Saturdays (if your tradition gathers on that day) or Sundays remain the ideal time for Sabbath keeping whenever possible.

Every Sabbath also serves as a taste of the glorious eternal party of music, food, and beauty that awaits us in heaven when we see him face to face (see Revelation 22:4). On every Sabbath, we experience a sampling of something greater that awaits us. Our short earthly lives are put in perspective as we look forward to the day when God's kingdom will come in all its fullness and we will enter an eternal Sabbath feast in God's perfect presence. We will taste his splendor, greatness, beauty, excellence, and glory far beyond anything we ever experienced or dreamed.

As with stopping, resting, and delighting, we will need to prepare in advance how to do this. Is it any wonder that the Jewish people traditionally had a Day of Preparation for the Sabbath? There was food to buy, clothes to wash for the children, and final preparations to be made.

What will it mean to prepare yourself for worship, to receive the

Word of God? What time do you need to go to bed the night before? When might you have times of silence and solitude or prayer during the day? What final items do you need to resolve so you can have an uncluttered Sabbath?

Devout Jews today have numerous customs related to their Friday Shabbat meal as a family. They maintain various traditions, from the lighting of candles to the reading of psalms to the blessing of children to the eating of the meal to the giving of thanks to God. Each is designed to keep God at the center of their Sabbath.[21]

There are an amazing variety of Sabbath possibilities before you. It is vitally important you keep in mind your unique life situation as you work out these four principles of Sabbath keeping into your life. Experiment. Make a plan. Follow it for one to two months. Then reflect back on what changes you would like to make. There is no one right way that works for every person.

Sabbath is like receiving the gift of a heavy snow day every week. Stores are closed. Roads are impassable. Suddenly you have the gift of a day to do whatever you want. You don't have any obligations, pressures, or responsibilities. You have permission to play, be with friends, take a nap, read a good book. Few of us would give ourselves a "no obligation day" very often.

God gives you one—every seventh day.

Think about it. He gives you over seven weeks (fifty-two days in all) of snow days every year! And if you begin to practice stopping, resting, delighting, and contemplating for one twenty-four-hour period each week, you will soon find your other six days becoming infused with those same qualities. I suspect that has always been God's plan.[22]

THE PRINCIPLE OF LONGER SABBATICALS

God knew that if Israel were to be true to her calling and purpose, they would need more than weekly Sabbaths. They would need longer stretches of time to stop, to rest, to delight in and contemplate him. For this reason God built into their national economic and political life entire Sabbatical *years*. God commanded all Israel to give the land a "Sabbath of rest" one year in every seven (see Leviticus 25:1–7). Since he knew this would require great faith, God promised that what they harvested in year six would be enough to feed them for two whole years. They were to trust God for his provision.[23]

These longer sabbaticals, too, are part of the rope God grants us to survive the blizzards of life. Consider the following applications for us today. First, each of us takes a vacation every year, for one, two, three, or more weeks. Consider viewing all or part of that time as a sabbatical. How might that change what you do and where you go? What might it look like for you to experience leisure away from work, with a God focus? One thing is for sure: none of us would return from our vacations in need of another vacation.

Second, consider participating for a few days at a spiritual retreat with a group or attending a training conference. Treat it as a sabbatical. You may want to simply go away overnight for a personal retreat with God every four to six months for a longer sabbatical. You may want to take some time from work to go on a mission trip to serve with a group from your church.

Third, if you are actively serving in a ministry at your church—whether it be as a small-group leader, a children's worker, a musician on the worship team, an usher—consider taking a rest after six or seven years. Even if you love it, do it. Take the time for a sabbatical *to* the Lord, not a vacation *from* church. Follow the same biblical principles applied to weekly Sabbaths. Prepare. Sketch out a plan. Talk it over with your pastor or a friend. Model a rhythm of life.

Finally, if you are a pastor or Christian leader I want to encourage you to take time for sabbatical rest every seven or eight years. To be providing leadership in God's church is a demanding task. The soil needs to be replenished and to lie dormant for a season. I have taken two three- to four-month sabbaticals eight years apart. They transformed my life, my marriage, and the church I pastor. I continue to feed others out of the rich fruit of those sabbaticals.

Geri jokes at times, "I have been married to four different men the last twenty-one years, all of them named Pete Scazzero, and New Life Fellowship Church has had at least four pastors, all of whom were Pete Scazzero."

GRIPPING THE ROPE DURING OUR BLIZZARDS

God invites us to grab on to his rope in the blizzard of life. He seeks to lead us back home to him. Sabbath keeping and the Daily Office summon us to slow down to God's rhythm. For when we are busier than what God requires, as Thomas Merton has written, we do violence to ourselves:

> There is a pervasive form of contemporary violence . . . activism and overwork. The rush and pressure of modern life are a form, perhaps the most common form, of its innate violence. To allow oneself to be carried away by a multitude of conflicting concerns, to surrender to too many demands, to commit oneself to too many projects, to want to help everyone in everything, is to succumb to violence. . . . It kills the root of inner wisdom which makes work fruitful.[24]

And in doing violence to ourselves, we are unable to love others in and through the love of Christ. This leads us to the topic of our next chapter: growing into an emotional adult who loves others well.

Lord, help me to grab hold of you as my rope in the blizzard today. I need you. The idea of stopping to be with you one, two, or three times a day seems overwhelming, but I know I need you. Show me the way. Teach me to be prayerfully attentive to you. This idea of Sabbath, Lord, will require a lot of change in the way I am living life. Lead me, Lord, in how to take the next step with this. Help me trust you with all that will remain unfinished, to not try to run your world for you. Set me free to begin reorienting my life around you and you alone. In Jesus' name, amen.

CHAPTER NINE

GROW INTO AN EMOTIONALLY MATURE ADULT

Learning New Skills to Love Well

In Dostoevsky's novel *The Brothers Karamazov*, a wealthy woman asks an elderly monk how she can know if God exists. He tells her no explanation or argument can achieve this, only the practice of "active love." She then confesses that sometimes she dreams about a life of loving service to others. At such times she thinks perhaps she will become a Sister of Mercy, live in holy poverty, and serve the poor in the humblest way. But then it crosses her mind how ungrateful some of the people she would serve are likely to be. They would probably complain that the soup she served wasn't hot enough or that the bread wasn't fresh enough or the bed was too hard. She confesses that she couldn't bear such ingratitude—and so her dreams about serving others vanish, and once again she finds herself wondering if there is a God.

To this the wise monk responds, "Love in practice is a harsh and dreadful thing compared to love in dreams."[1]

Loving well is the goal of the Christian life. This is easier in our dreams than in practice. It requires that we grow into emotional adulthood in Christ, the rewards of which are rich beyond measure.

THE PROBLEM OF EMOTIONAL IMMATURITY

Many people know the truths of the Bible relatively well. They can recite many of the Ten Commandments and articulate key principles for Christian living. They believe wholeheartedly they should be living them. The problem is they don't know how!

The following is one simple, common scenario:

Jessica is a gifted manager in her company. She has been a Christian for fifteen years and loves spending time with God. When the vice president of her company was making schedules for managers to meet with clients out of town, he asked Jessica to pick the weeks she would prefer to travel over the next three months. Within the week Jessica e-mailed him the dates and eagerly awaited his confirmation. None arrived. Jessica called his office the following week.

His administrative assistant answered. "Well, according to the schedule I have in front of me, the next three months are all full," she said. "I guess this means he doesn't need you right now. But thanks for calling."

Jessica sat stunned in her chair. "Thank you," she replied robotically and hung up.

For the next two weeks Jessica wrestled with God and herself. She asked God for forgiveness for the anger she was feeling. She tried to figure out why the vice president had changed his mind. She humbled herself to God. She cried out in prayer for love toward her coworkers. She lost sleep.

Finally, she concluded God was dealing with her stubborn self-will.

Over time Jessica distanced herself from the vice president and other managers, avoiding them whenever possible. During the next two years she worked hard, but she felt like she had hit a ceiling in how far she could go with this company. Eventually, she took a position with another company.

Jessica is committed to her personal relationship with Jesus Christ. She practices spiritual disciplines. The problem, however, is that her commitment to Jesus Christ does not include relating to people in an emotionally mature way. Instead, she misapplies biblical truth and follows, most probably, the relational skills learned unconsciously in her family growing up.

What assumptions is she making about her vice president? His administrative assistant? About God's will for her life? What might she have done to prevent her pain? To preserve her relationships at work?

Unless Jessica receives equipping in this area, she will likely repeat the same pattern over and over again.

We learn many skills to be competent in our careers and at school. We don't learn, however, the skills necessary to grow into an emotionally mature adult who loves well. The Bible is clear what we are to do. Part of growing into an emotionally mature Christian is learning how to apply practically and effectively the truths we believe. For example:

- How can I be quick to hear and slow to speak?
- How can I be angry and not sin?
- How can I watch my heart above all else (since that is the place from which life flows)?
- How can I speak the truth in love?
- How can I be a true peacemaker?
- How can I mourn?
- How can I not bear false witness against my neighbor?
- How can I get rid of all bitterness, rage, and envy?

The end result of an inability to walk out our beliefs is that our churches and relationships within the church are not qualitatively any different from the world around us.

EMOTIONAL INFANTS, CHILDREN, ADOLESCENTS, AND ADULTS

Jesus preached great messages to the multitudes. Yet he knew that would not be enough for people to truly "get it." So he chose twelve disciples with whom he lived day and night for three years. He modeled how his teaching worked out practically. He had them practice. He supervised. He imparted power.

Jesus knew inspiration was not enough.[2]

I have spent all my adult life giving inspiring sermons about God's heart for us to love people. I have preached messages about how Jesus saw each human being as infinitely precious and a treasure in God's sight. I have quoted Mother Teresa of Calcutta's inspiring quote about "loving one person at a time," and Thomas Merton's revelation that people "were walking around shining like the sun."[3] But I have found that telling people to love better and more is not enough. They need practical skills incorporated into their spiritual formation to grow out of emotional infancy into emotional adulthood. It is easy to grow physically into a chronological adult. It is quite another to grow into an emotional adult. Many people may be, chronologically, forty-five years old but remain an emotional infant, child, or adolescent.

The question then is: how do I distinguish between them? The following is a brief summary of each:[4]

EMOTIONAL INFANTS

- Look for others to take care of them
- Have great difficulty entering into the world of others
- Are driven by need for instant gratification
- Use others as objects to meet their needs

EMOTIONAL CHILDREN

- Are content and happy as long as they receive what they want
- Unravel quickly from stress, disappointments, trials
- Interpret disagreements as personal offenses
- Are easily hurt
- Complain, withdraw, manipulate, take revenge, become sarcastic when they don't get their way
- Have great difficulty calmly discussing their needs and wants in a mature, loving way

EMOTIONAL ADOLESCENTS

- Tend to often be defensive
- Are threatened and alarmed by criticism
- Keep score of what they give so they can ask for something later in return

- Deal with conflict poorly, often blaming, appeasing, going to a third party, pouting, or ignoring the issue entirely
- Become preoccupied with themselves
- Have great difficulty truly listening to another person's pain, disappointments, or needs
- Are critical and judgmental

EMOTIONAL ADULTS

- Are able to ask for what they need, want, or prefer—clearly, directly, honestly
- Recognize, manage, and take responsibility for their own thoughts and feelings
- Can, when under stress, state their own beliefs and values without becoming adversarial
- Respect others without having to change them
- Give people room to make mistakes and not be perfect
- Appreciate people for who they are—the good, bad, and ugly—not for what they give back
- Accurately assess their own limits, strengths, and weaknesses and are able to freely discuss them with others
- Are deeply in tune with their own emotional world and able to enter into the feelings, needs, and concerns of others without losing themselves
- Have the capacity to resolve conflict maturely and negotiate solutions that consider the perspectives of others

THE SPIRITUAL DISCIPLINE OF PRACTICING THE PRESENCE OF PEOPLE

As emotionally mature Christian adults, we recognize that loving well is the essence of true spirituality. This requires that we experience connection with God, with ourselves, and with other people. God invites us to practice his presence in our daily lives. At the same time, he invites us "to practice the presence of people," within an awareness of his presence, in our daily relationships.[5] The two are rarely brought together.

Jesus' profound, contemplative prayer life with his Father resulted in a contemplative presence with people. Love is "to reveal the beauty of another person to themselves," wrote Jean Vanier.[6] Jesus did that with each person he met. This ability to really listen and pay attention to people was at the very heart of his mission. It could not help but move him to compassion. In the same way, out of our contemplative time with God, we, too, are invited to be prayerfully present to people, revealing their beauty to themselves.

The religious leaders of Jesus' day, the "church leaders" of that time, never made that connection. They were diligent, zealous, and absolutely committed to having God as Lord of their lives. They memorized the entire books of Genesis, Exodus, Leviticus, Numbers, and Deuteronomy. They prayed five times a day. They tithed all their income and gave money to the poor. They evangelized. But they never delighted in people. They did not link loving God with the need to be diligent, zealous, and absolutely committed to growing in their ability to love people. For this reason they criticized Jesus repeatedly for being a "glutton and a drunkard, a friend of tax collectors and 'sinners'" (Matthew 11:19). He delighted in people and life too much.

Jesus refused to separate the practice of the presence of God from the practice of the presence of people. When pushed to the wall to separate this unbreakable union, Jesus refused. He summarized the entire Bible for us: "'Love the Lord your God with all your heart and with all your soul and with all your mind.' This is the first and greatest commandment. And the second is like it: 'Love your neighbor as yourself.' All the Law and the Prophets hang on these two commandments" (Matthew 22:37–40).

OUR GREAT PROBLEM

I can't help but experience life with me at the center of my universe. With my eyes I look out on the world. With my ears I hear what is going on. I can only feel, want, and experience what I am feeling, wanting, and experiencing. I naturally want the people around me to give up themselves and become what I want them to be. I prefer those close to me to think, feel, and act toward the world in the same way I do. I prefer the illusion of sameness when really we are very different from each other. I want other people's worlds to be like mine. I even act the same way in my relationship with God, walking out my spirituality as if I am the center of the universe.

For this reason, M. Scott Peck argues that we are all born narcissists and that learning to grow out of our narcissism is at the heart of the spiritual journey.[7]

When Geri and I were married we lit what is recognized today as the unity candle. There were two separate candles representing our separate lives. After taking our vows, we lit a third candle and extinguished the two separate ones. This symbolized we were now "one."

"We are one," we proclaimed to our family and friends.

The question we didn't answer was: "Which one?" For the first nine years of our marriage, I unconsciously answered that question with: "Yes, Geri and I are one, and I *am* the one!"

To grow spiritually a Copernican revolution must take place in the way we perceive ourselves in relation to others. When Copernicus removed human beings from the center of the universe and said we revolve around the sun, not vice versa, it sent a shock wave through Western civilization. To discover the "otherness" of a spouse, friend, boss, child, and coworker and to see them as separate, unique human beings—without losing yourself—is also a Copernican revolution of emotional maturity.

I-It Relationships

In 1923, the great Jewish theologian Martin Buber wrote a brilliant but difficult to read book, called *I and Thou*.[8] Buber described the most healthy or mature relationship possible between two human beings as an "I-Thou" relationship. In such a relationship I recognize that I am made in the image of God and so is every other person on the face of the earth. This makes them a "Thou" to me. Because of that reality, every person deserves respect—that is, I treat them with dignity and worth. I do not dehumanize or objectify them. I affirm them as having a unique and separate existence apart from me.

See the following circles illustrations:

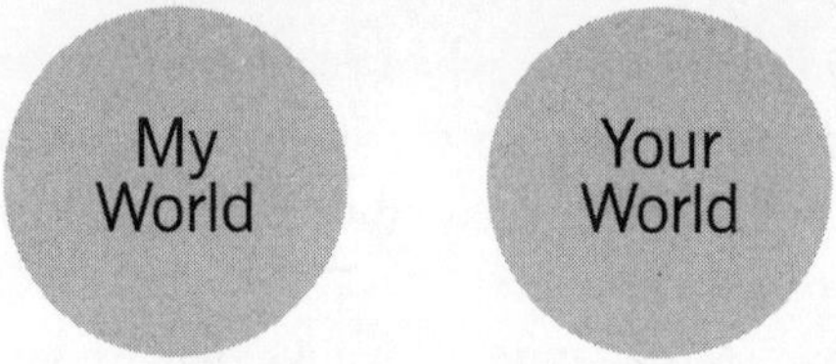

Though you are different from me—a "You" or "Thou"—I still respect, love, and value you.

Buber argued that in most of our human relationships we lose sight of others as separate from us. We treat people as objects, as an "It" (to use Buber's word). In the I-It relationship I treat you as a means to an end—as we might use a toothbrush or car.

What might that look like?

- I walk in and dump my work on my secretary without saying hello.
- I move people around on an organizational chart at a staff meeting as if they were objects or subhuman.
- I talk about people in authority as if they were subhuman.
- I treat Geri or our children as if they are not in charge of their own freedom, dreams, autonomy; I expect them to be the picture I have of them in my head.
- I am threatened when someone disagrees with my political views.
- I listen to my neighbors' problems and help them with chores around their house hoping they will attend the Christmas outreach at our church. They don't . . . and I move on to someone else.

The result of I-It relationships is that I get frustrated when people don't fit into my plans. The way I see things is "right." And if you don't see it as I do, you are not seeing things the "right" way. You are wrong.

Recognizing the uniqueness and separateness of every other person on earth is so pivotal to emotional maturity. We so easily demand that people view the world the way we do. We believe our way is *the* right way.

Augustine defined sin as the state of being "caved in on oneself."

Instead of using our God-given power to orient ourselves to God and other human beings, we focus inward. For this reason when Dante, in his famous *Inferno*, arrived at the very pit of hell, ice dominated, not fire. The coldness spoke of the death, the inwardness, the coldness of sin. Satan was stuck, frozen in ice, and weeping from all six of his eyes.[9] C. S. Lewis described hell in *The Great Divorce* as a place where each person lives in isolation, millions of miles apart from one another, because they can't get along.[10]

I-Thou Relationships

True relationships, said Buber, can only exist between two people willing to connect across their differences. God fills that in-between space of an I-Thou relationship. God not only can be glimpsed in genuine dialogue but penetrates their in-between space. See the following diagram:

The central tenet of Buber's life work was that the I-Thou relationship between persons intimately reflects the I-Thou relationship humans have with God. Genuine relationship with any Thou shows traces of the "eternal Thou."[11] For this reason, when we love someone well as emotional adults, treating them as a Thou, not an It, it is such a powerful experience. When genuine love is released in a relationship, God's presence is manifest. The separate space between us becomes sacred space.

Jessica's relationship with her vice president was not what Buber would characterize as I-Thou. Jessica did not have the skills and emotional maturity to resolve this conflict maturely. She also did not have the ability to state her own feelings and beliefs without thinking adversarially. The end result was an isolation and coldness in her relationships at work that resembled hell more than heaven.

EMOTIONAL MATURITY AND CONFLICT

Practicing the "I-Thou" in our relationships leads to another aspect of emotional maturity. It informs our capacity to resolve conflicts maturely and negotiate solutions as we consider other people's perspectives.

At the heart of true peacemaking is acknowledgment, once again, that we are human beings made in God's image. Likeness to our Creator, along with Christ's example, puts us on paths that desire to live in the truth and not in pretense, even when that means a conflict may result. Yet most Christians I meet are poor at resolving conflict. There are at least two reasons for this: the first relates to wrong beliefs about peacemaking and the second relates to a lack of training and equipping in this area.

Ignoring Conflict—False Peacemaking

A tragically misinterpreted verse in the New Testament is Jesus' proclamation: "Blessed are the peacemakers, for they will be called sons of God" (Matthew 5:9). Most people think that Jesus calls us in this verse to be pacifiers and appeasers who ensure that nobody gets upset. We are to keep the peace, ignoring difficult issues and problems, making sure things remain stable and serene.

When, out of fear, we avoid conflict and appease people, we are false peacemakers. For example:

Karl is upset about the behavior of his spouse who constantly comes home later after work. He says nothing. Why? He thinks he is being like Christ by not saying anything, although he does give her a cold shoulder. He is a false peacemaker.

Pam disagrees with her coworkers at lunch when they slander her boss. She is afraid to speak up. She goes along. *I don't want to kill the atmosphere by speaking up and disagreeing*, she thinks. She is a false peacemaker.

Bob goes to dinner with ten other people. He is tight financially, so he orders only a salad and appetizer. Meanwhile, the other nine order appetizers, steak, wine, and desserts. When the bill comes, someone says, "Let's divide up the bill equally. It will take forever to figure it out." Everyone agrees. Bob is dying on the inside but won't say anything. He is a false peacemaker.

Yolanda is engaged. She would like more time to rethink her decision but is afraid that her fiancé and his family will get angry. She goes through with the wedding. She is a false peacemaker.

Ellen loves her parents. They are both quite critical about how she raises her children. Each holiday is filled with tension. Ellen doesn't say anything because she doesn't want to hurt their feelings. She is a false peacemaker.

Sharon thinks her boyfriend is irresponsible but feels bad for him. *He has had so much pain already in his life*, she thinks. *How can I add to that?* So she backs down from telling him the truth about the way his behavior is slowly killing their relationship. The relationship dies a slow death. She is a false peacemaker.

The problem with all these scenarios is that the way of true peace will never come through pretending what is wrong is right! True peacemakers love God, others, and themselves enough to disrupt false peace. Jesus models this for us.

Embracing Conflict—The Path to True Peace

Conflict and trouble were central to the mission of Jesus. He disrupted the false peace all around him—in the lives of his disciples, the crowds, the religious leaders, the Romans, those buying and selling in the temple. He taught that true peacemaking disrupts false peace even in families: "Do not suppose that I have come to bring peace to the earth. I did not come to bring peace, but a sword. For I have come to turn 'a man against his father, a daughter against her mother, a daughter-in-law against her mother-in-law—a man's enemies will be the members of his own household'" (Matthew 10:34–36).

Why? You can't have the true peace of Christ's kingdom with lies and pretense. They must be exposed to the light and replaced with the truth. This is the mature, loving thing to do.

In the Beatitudes, Jesus explains to us the characteristics we need to display if we are to engage in true peacemaking—poverty of spirit, meekness, purity of heart, mercy, etc. (Matthew 5:3–11). He also follows the call to true peacemaking by stating that persecution will follow for those of us who follow him in this.

Nonetheless, unresolved conflicts are one of the greatest tensions in Christians' lives today. Most of us hate them. We don't know what to do with them. Instead of risking any more broken relationships, we prefer to ignore the difficult issues and settle for a "false peace," hoping against hope they will somehow go away. They don't. And we all learn, sooner or later, that you can't build Christ's kingdom on lies and pretense. Only the truth will do.

LEARNING SKILLS TO BE TRUE PEACEMAKERS

Many of us believe loving well is learned automatically, that it is just a "feeling." We underestimate the depth of our bad habits and what is needed to sustain long-term, Christlike change in our relationships.

This belief led Geri and me, over eleven years ago, to begin learning from a variety of sources, gathering exercises and tools, so people could learn how to practice the I-Thou with others. Our desire was to help followers of Jesus obey the command to love well. We wanted to move people from defensiveness, reactivity, and fear to openness, empathy, and vulnerability. We realized they needed to experience a new kingdom-way of relating that was outside their comfort zone. Practicing new skills like the ones that follow will cause a level of discomfort initially. They are easy to understand but difficult to implement. But by repeatedly practicing mature, godly behaviors, we have seen people freed from lifelong cycles of emotional immaturity.[12] They have served as a helpful link in moving people into becoming mothers and fathers of the faith.

We have collected a number of tools and exercises. The following, however, are a few we use in all kinds of relationships—our marriage, parenting, staff team, and wider church. They each provide, in their own way, a means to help people move out of an I-It way of relating to others into an I-Thou relationship. They each, in their own way, contribute to helping us follow Christ in becoming true peacemakers and lead us to love well.

Speaking and Listening

Speaking and listening is the essence of having an I-Thou relationship with another person. Everyone knows that communication is essential to all relationships. People take courses in high school, college, and beyond to learn more about it. Yet few people do it well. This is especially true under stress and in conflict.

For many of us, our childhood was an experience of invisibility. For this reason, simply being the speaker and expressing your wishes and hopes can be a very healing, powerful experience. Moreover, this process of speaking and listening creates a fresh connection between two people, slowing them both down.

I encourage you to see the following structure as a spiritual practice of meeting God through your time with this person. Ask God to help you be prayerfully present. Ask him to help you receive this person as if they were Jesus. How might Jesus Christ want to come to you through this person? Ask God to clear the noise from your mind so you can be still enough to enter the speaker's world.

AS THE SPEAKER

- Talk about *your* own thoughts, *your* own feelings (speak in the "I").
- Be brief. Use short sentences or phrases.
- Correct the other person if you believe he or she has missed something.
- Continue speaking until you feel you've been understood.
- When you don't have anything else to say, say, "That's all for now."

AS THE LISTENER

- Put your own agenda on hold. Be quiet and still as you would before God.
- Allow the other person to speak until he or she completes a thought.
- Reflect accurately the other person's words back to him or her. You have two options: paraphrase in a way the other

person agrees is accurate or use his or her own words.
- When it appears the speaker is done, ask, "Is there more?"

The purpose of repeating back what the other person says is to be sure you are hearing them accurately. This requires you as the listener to put your ideas and responses on hold. Validate the other person, letting them know that you really see and understand his or her world and point of view. You recognize they are different. Typical validation phrases might include: "That makes sense . . ." or "I can see that because . . ." or "I can understand that because . . ."

The Bill of Rights[13]

Respect is not a feeling. It is how we treat another person. Regardless of how we might feel about another human being, they are made in God's image and of infinite value and worth. The following Bill of Rights has remained posted on our refrigerator and in our lives for years. Next to each "right" are examples from our family's life.

BILL OF RIGHTS

Respect means I give myself and others the right to:

- *Space and privacy* (e.g., knocking on doors before entering, not opening one another's mail, respecting each other's needs for quiet and space);
- *Be different* (e.g., allowing preferences for food, movies, volume of music, and how we spend our time);
- *Disagree* (e.g., making room for each person to think and see life differently);
- *Be heard* (e.g., listening to each other's desires, opinions, thoughts, feelings, etc.);
- *Be taken seriously* (e.g., listening and being present to one another);
- *Be given the benefit of the doubt* (e.g., checking out assumptions rather than judging one another when misunderstandings arise);

- *Be told the truth* (e.g., counting on the truth when asking each other for information—from "Did you study for the test that you failed?" to "Why were you late coming home?");
- *Be consulted* (e.g., checking and asking when decisions will affect others);
- *Be imperfect and make mistakes* (e.g., leaving "room" for breaking things, forgetting things, letting each other down unintentionally, failing tests when we have studied, etc.);
- *Courteous and honorable treatment* (e.g., using words that don't hurt, asking before using, consulting when appropriate, treating each other as I-Thou's); and
- *Be respected* (e.g., taking one another's feelings into account)

Checking Out Assumptions[14]

The ninth commandment reads: "You shall not give false testimony against your neighbor" (Exodus 20:16). Checking out assumptions is a very simple, but powerful tool that eliminates untold numbers of conflicts in relationships. It enables me to check out whether what I'm thinking or feeling about you is true. It enables me to clarify potential misunderstandings.

Every time I make an assumption about someone who has hurt or disappointed me without confirming it, I believe a lie about this person in my head. This assumption is a misrepresentation of reality. Because I have not checked it out with the other person, it is very possible I am believing something untrue. It is also likely I will pass that false assumption around to others.

When we leave reality for a mental creation of our own doing (hidden assumptions), we create a counterfeit world. When we do this, it can properly be said that we exclude God from our lives because God does not exist outside of reality and truth. In doing so we wreck relationships by creating endless confusion and conflict. Jessica, in our opening illustration of this chapter, made all sorts of assumptions about why the boss failed to schedule her to meet with clients. The Bible has much to say about not taking on the role of judge to others (see Matthew 7:1–5).

Following are some important steps in using this tool with another person:

- Reflect on something you suspect the other person thinks or feels but hasn't told you.
- Ask: "Do I have your permission to check out an assumption I am making?" (If he or she grants it, then you can proceed.)
- Say: "I think you think . . ." or "I assume you are thinking . . ." (fill in the blank). When you finish, ask them: "Is this correct?"
- Give the other person an opportunity to respond.

You can use this with employees, employers, spouses, friends, roommates, coworkers, parents, children. The list is endless.

Expectations[15]

Unmet and unclear expectations create havoc in our places of employment, classrooms, friendships, dating relationships, marriages, sports teams, families, and churches. For example:

- Of course you're coming to the family event. We're important to you, aren't we?
- I never knew the job involved all that. You never told me.
- My adult son should know I need him to come over and fix things. I shouldn't have to ask.
- I'm so disillusioned. I expected that a good marriage just happened naturally.
- I'm the only one caring for my aging parents. My siblings expect me to do everything.
- If she really cared about me, she would call me.
- In a good church everyone should be friendly and supportive when someone is hurting.

We expect other people to know what we want before we say it (especially if they are invested in the relationship). The problem with most expectations is that they are:

- unconscious—we have expectations we're not even aware of until someone disappoints us;
- unrealistic—we may have illusions about others. For example, we think a spouse, a friend, or a pastor will be available at all times to meet our needs;
- unspoken—we may have never told our spouse, friend, or employee what we expect, yet we are angry when our expectations are not met; and
- un-agreed upon—we may have had our own thoughts about what was expected, but it was never agreed upon by the other person.

Expectations are only valid when they have been mutually agreed upon. We all know the unpleasant experience of other people having expectations we never agreed to.

In order for expectations to be established, they must first be:

- conscious (I have to become aware of the expectations I have for the other person);
- realistic (I have to ask myself if my expectations regarding the other person are realistic);
- spoken (I have to speak my expectations clearly, directly, and respectfully to the other person); and
- agreed upon (in order for my expectations to be valid, the other person must be aware of and agree to them; otherwise it is simply a hope).

Think of an expectation you have of a spouse, friend, roommate, boss, family member, or coworker. Ask yourself: Am I conscious of what it is? Is it realistic? Has it been spoken? Have they also agreed to this? Initiate conversation with them and seek to come to a mutually agreed upon expectation. Now think of a person who may have an unconscious, unrealistic, unspoken, and un-agreed upon expectation of you. Sit down with them and discuss it. Seek to come to a mutually agreed upon expectation.

Allergies and Triggers

We are familiar with physical allergies to certain foods or pollen, but less familiar with our emotional allergies. An emotional allergy is an intense reaction to something in the present that reminds us, consciously or unconsciously, of an event from our history.

Examples of emotional allergies might be the response I used to have when Geri wanted to go away for weekends with her girlfriends in the early years of our marriage. I would have an allergic reaction. It reminded me of early feelings of my parents' emotional unavailability. The circumstances were very different, but the feeling was the same.

Another example is when Theresa sees her husband watching television instead of parenting the children with her and she gets very angry. She attacks and belittles him because he unconsciously reminds her of her father who left her home when she was seven years old, leaving her and her mom to fend for themselves.

As you can see, what happens most often in an allergic reaction is that we end up treating the person with whom we are in a relationship now as if they were someone from our past. We treat them like an It.

The PAIRS organization has developed a helpful exercise ("Healing the Ledger") we encourage people to take part in, either with another person or by themselves:[16]

- An emotional allergy you trigger in me is . . .
- When this allergy happens, what I think or tell myself is . . .
- When this allergy happens, I feel . . .
- When this allergy happens, what I think and feel about myself for even having these feelings is . . .
- When this happens inside me, the behavior you then see from me is . . .
- What this allergy relates to in my history is . . .
- When this allergy happens, you remind me of . . .
- The price we are paying for this in our relationship is . . .
- The words from the past that I needed, the words that I wish had been said to me, are . . .

Many people realize through this exercise how much they still live in the past and project it into present relationships. Once we begin to see this connection, we can begin making different choices that are more loving, emotionally adult responses rather than allergic reactions.

THE CHURCH AS A NEW CULTURE

One of the greatest gifts we can give our world is to be a community of emotionally healthy adults who love well. This will take the power of God and a commitment to learn, grow, and break with unhealthy, destructive patterns that go back generations in our families and cultures—and in some cases, our Christian culture also.

Remember, Jesus formed a community with a small group from Galilee, a backward province in Palestine. They were neither spiritually nor emotionally mature. Peter, the point leader, had a big problem with his mouth and was a bundle of contradictions. Andrew, his brother, was quiet and behind the scenes. James and John were given the name "sons of thunder" because they were aggressive, hotheaded, ambitious, and intolerant. Philip was skeptical and negative. He had limited vision. "We can't do that," summed up his faith when confronted by the problem of feeding the five thousand. Nathanael Bartholemew was prejudiced and opinionated. Matthew was the most hated person in Capernaum, working in a profession that abused innocent people. Thomas was melancholy, mildly depressive, and pessimistic. James, son of Alphaeus, and Judas, son of James, were nobodies. The Bible says nothing about them. Simon the Zealot was a freedom fighter and terrorist in his day. Judas, the treasurer, was a thief and a loner. He pretended to be loyal to Jesus before finally betraying him.

Most of them, however, did have one great quality: they were willing. That is all God asks of us.

In the next chapter, we will bring the entire book together as we look at creating a "rule of life" for our lives to enable us to walk out all we have talked about so far. So stay with me.

Lord Jesus Christ, Son of God, have mercy on me. I am aware, Lord, of how often I treat people as Its, as objects, instead of looking at them with the eyes and heart of Christ. Lord, I have unhealthy ways of relating that are deeply imbedded in me. Please change me. Make me a vessel to spread mature, steady, reliable love so that people with whom I come in contact sense your tenderness and kindness. Deliver me from false peacemaking that is driven by fear. Lord Jesus, help me love well like you. Grow me, I pray, into an emotionally mature adult through the Holy Spirit's power. In Jesus' name, amen.

CHAPTER TEN

GO THE NEXT STEP TO DEVELOP A "RULE OF LIFE"

Loving Christ Above All Else

In *The Book of the Dun Cow*, Walter Wangerin creates a fantasy world of animals living in community around a chicken coop. Chauntecleer, the rooster of the coop, is the leader in charge of guiding the other animals who depend on him. The peace of the kingdom is broken when Ultimate Evil, in the form of Wyrm, threatens to destroy the coop community through the release of "licorice-length black and poisonous snakes." The community is held together by Chauntecleer as he crows the Daily Office, a gift he has received and disciplined out of the memory of his own history. He will eventually use force and violence to destroy Wyrm. But in this battle against evil, the community around the chicken coop is only able to fight because of their faith and the spiritual exercises they practice, all of which appear on the surface to be a waste of time against such enormous evil.

We, too, are called to order our lives around spiritual practices and disciplines—that is, a "Rule of Life," something utterly foreign to the world around us. It is a call to order our entire life in such a way that the love of Christ comes before all else. And in doing so, like Chauntecleer, the very quality of our lives holds the possibility of being transformed into a gift to our families, friends, coworkers, and communities.

THE ANCIENT TREASURE OF A RULE OF LIFE

Please don't be intimidated by the word *rule*. The word comes from the Greek for "trellis." A trellis is a tool that enables a grapevine to get off the ground and grow upward, becoming more fruitful and productive. In the same way, a Rule of Life is a trellis that helps us abide in Christ and become more fruitful spiritually.[1]

A Rule of Life, very simply, is an intentional, conscious plan to keep God at the center of everything we do. It provides guidelines to help us continually remember God as the Source of our lives. It includes our unique combination of spiritual practices that provide structure and direction for us to intentionally pay attention and remember God in everything we do. The starting point and foundation of any Rule is a desire to be with God and to love him.

Very few people have a conscious plan for developing their spiritual lives. Most Christians are not intentional, but rather functional, like cars on autopilot. Our crammed schedules, endless to-do lists, demanding jobs and families, constant noise, information bombardment, and anxieties keep us speeding up, not slowing down. We have routines to manage other parts of our lives. For example, each morning we may get up, feed the cat, then make coffee, exercise, get dressed for work, and eat breakfast.

The reality, however, is that every person has an unconscious Rule for developing his or her spiritual life. We each have our values and ways of doing things. This may include, for example, attending a church on Sundays, participating in a small group, serving in a ministry, and/or ten minutes for prayer and Bible reading before going to bed.

However, our present spiritual practices are not enough to keep us afloat in the ocean of the beast, the Babylon of our twenty-first-century world. Fighting against such a strong current, without the anchor of a Rule of Life, is almost impossible. Eventually we find ourselves unfocused, distracted, and adrift spiritually.

Is it any wonder that most people live off other people's spirituality rather than taking the time to develop their own direct experience of God? Most Christians talk about prayer but don't pray. Most believe the Bible as the Word of God but have little idea what it says. Our goals for our children differ little from those of "pagans" who do not know God. Like the world, we, too, grade people based on their education, wealth, beauty, and popularity.

Nurturing a growing spirituality with depth in our present-day culture will require a thoughtful, conscious, intentional plan for our spiritual lives. To plan well, however, requires we go back to Daniel and early church history to consider the roots of this hidden treasure.

DANIEL'S "RULE OF LIFE"

Nebuchadnezzar and his Babylonian armies, with their gods, conquered Jerusalem and carried off most of the city's inhabitants as slaves. One of those was a young teenager named Daniel. Cut off from his family, teachers, friends, food, culture, and language, Daniel was brought into the Babylonian court of the king and sent to the best university in the land. He studied a completely foreign and pagan way of viewing the world—history, mathematics, medicine, religion, literature. He learned about myths, astrology, sorcery, and magic—all things banned in Israel. Pagan priests and counselors educated him in their wisdom and religion. In Babylon's effort to assimilate Daniel, they even changed his name.

Babylon had one simple goal: to eliminate Daniel's distinctiveness as a God follower and absorb him into the values of their culture.

How did Daniel resist the enormous power of Babylon? He was not a cloistered monk living behind walls. He had heavy job responsibilities with people giving him orders. He had a minimal support system, and, I imagine, a very long to-do list each day.

What Daniel did have was a plan, a Rule of Life. He did not leave the development of his interior life to chance. He knew "going to church on Sundays, along with a fifteen-minute daily quiet time" would never be enough. He knew what he was up against. While we know little of the specifics, it is clear that he oriented his entire life around loving God. He renounced certain activities, such as eating the king's contaminated food (see Daniel 1) and engaged in others, such as the Daily Office (see Daniel 6). Daniel somehow fed himself spiritually and blossomed into an extraordinary man of God in this hostile environment. He knew resisting the beast of Babylon and thriving required a plan that would enable him to pay attention to God.

A SHORT HISTORY OF THE "RULE"

From the end of the third century to the fifth century, men and women withdrew from society into the deserts of Egypt, Syria, Palestine, and Arabia to seek God. They wanted to free themselves from any distractions between them and God. A number of these monks later formed communities and organized their daily life around an agreed-upon plan consisting of work, prayer, and study of Scripture. They called this plan a Rule of Life.

Pachomius (A.D. 290–345) wrote the first known "Rule of Life" for his monastic communities in Egypt. Others followed with shorter and longer rules. Spiritual seekers from the Western church, most notably John Cassian, learned from these Desert Fathers and returned home to develop their own Rule of Life. Finally, this climaxed with Benedict (A.D. 480–547), who wrote the most widely known of monastic rules: the Rule of St. Benedict. The Rule of St. Benedict has not only shaped Western monasticism for the last fifteen hundred years, but continues to guide tens of thousands of people around the world today from all church traditions.

The great, buried gift in a Rule of Life is its goal of regulating our entire lives in such a way that we truly prefer the love of Christ above all things.

GETTING STARTED—THE BIG PICTURE

God has made each of us unique and different. Our goal is the same:

union with God in Christ, transformation into his image, and the freeing of our hearts from anything that stands in the way of Christ living in and through us. How we get there will vary, depending on our personality, gift mix, temperament, geographic location, and particular calling from God. In addition, God will have different practices and emphases at different seasons and phases of our lives.

St. Francis of Assisi, for example, would spend weeks alone in his hermitage and then travel for weeks preaching the message of Jesus to anyone who would listen.

Catherine Doherty helped develop Madonna Houses where members spent three days each week alone with God in *poustinias* (the Russian word for "desert"), and four days out serving the people.[2]

While an infinite number of variations exist for a Rule of Life, I like to see a panoramic view of the big picture first. The following is a suggested list of twelve elements (which I explain in greater detail in the next section) to consider as you begin to develop your personal Rule of Life.

PRAYER

1. Scripture
2. Silence and Solitude
3. Daily Office (Prayer)
4. Study

REST

5. Sabbath
6. Simplicity
7. Play and Recreation

WORK/ACTIVITY

8. Service and Mission
9. Care for the Physical Body

RELATIONSHIPS

10. Emotional Health

11. Family
12. Community (Companions for the Journey)

You may want to add new elements (e.g., hospitality) and/or delete others. I have placed the elements under four broad categories—Prayer, Rest, Work, and Relationships. You may prefer to place Study, for example, under Rest or Work. Or you may favor placing Care for the Physical Body under the category of Rest. The choice is yours.

Developing an intentional Rule of Life takes trial and error. You will need to learn a great deal about yourself as well as about each foundational area mentioned above. For example, what kinds of spiritual practices bring you closer to God? Which drive you away from him? How can you discern the right combination for your particular Rule of Life?

My personal Rule of Life is a constantly changing document. It is a "live" work in progress—always. For example, due to my highly intuitive, conscientious temperament, I rarely write down my goals and commitments. For me, it can easily become a "have to" rather than a "want to" out of love for Christ.

Give yourself lots of time for the slow development of what works best for you. As you examine your life, you may notice many areas that need work. The best approach is to start with only one or two elements for the first few months. Then, after you experience some success with those, you will want to add another building block to your Rule. Or you may want to stay with the same element to work on over a long period of time. An example under Prayer might look something like this:

- Pray the Jesus prayer ("Lord Jesus Christ, Son of God, have mercy on me, a sinner") each day at work, several times a day.
- Take fifteen minutes for silence at lunch three times a week.
- Practice the Ignatian prayer of examen three nights a week before going to bed.
- Fast for one meal every Wednesday during Lent.

If possible, find a companion for this journey. It may be a spiritual director, a mentor, a trusted friend, a mature Christian, or a small group. This will serve to keep you on track.

Don't be hard on yourself. St. Benedict writes at the beginning of his Rule of Life:

> Therefore we intend to establish a school for the Lord's service . . . . Do not be daunted immediately by fear and run away from the road that leads to salvation. It is bound to be narrow at the outset. But as we progress in this way of life and in faith, we shall run on the path of God's commandments, our hearts overflowing with the inexpressible delight of love.[3]

THE ELEMENTS OF A RULE OF LIFE

Scripture

God speaks to us in and through the Word. Your plan during one season of your life may be reading through the Bible in a year or following the lectionary of Scripture readings from the Book of Common Prayer. In recent years I have moved to a reflective meditation on smaller portions of Scripture. *Lectio divina*, the ancient practice of contemplative reading, has become a weekly practice for me. This begins with reading a short passage of Scripture and then reflecting on it, allowing it to quietly work on you, as leaven in bread or water on a stone. The key is to read slowly, chewing over the words and allowing them to feed and transform you. This has led me also to prayerfully memorize small portions of Scripture each week.

Silence and Solitude

It is said of Abbot Agathon, one of the Desert Fathers: "For three years he carried a stone in his mouth until he learned to be silent." I think I could use a few good rocks myself! This is one of the most challenging and least practiced disciplines among Christians today. When we are silent, we come face-to-face with our addiction to being in control and always trying to fix things. As Dallas Willard says, "Silence is frightening because it strips us as nothing else does, throwing us upon the stark realities of our life. It reminds us of death, which will cut us off from this world and leave only us and God."[4]

I often integrate my times of silence into the Daily Office each day. I seek to take between five and twenty minutes, a few times a week, to "be still before the LORD and wait patiently for him" (Psalm 37:7). This continues to be the core of my cutting edge for growing in Christ.

Daily Office

As you read in the previous chapter, this spiritual practice has a rich history in both Scripture and church history. I need structure, spontaneity, and variety in the way I approach the Daily Office each day. For example, I often use Phyllis Tickle's *Divine Hours* to provide me with a skeletal structure for morning, midday, and evening prayer and compline. I continue to use the Book of Common Prayer's lectionary for reading through the psalms each day. I love praying the psalms as the central part of my Daily Office. I also like having a devotional classic available as part of my morning Office each day. Many people pray with nature, setting aside time in silence to examine a leaf, a flower, a tree, the grass, the sky, giving God praise for his creation.[5]

Study

Few people recognize that spending intentional time reading and studying is a spiritual discipline. Yet these, too, are an important way of encountering God in new ways. One of the most striking features of the Rule of St. Benedict is that three hours a day were set aside for reading and reflection. He didn't say someone should be sent around the monastery to see if people were doing their work. But he did want someone to go around seeing if the monks were doing their reading and study! And this was in A.D. 550 when many of the monks had to learn to read first! Benedict understood an important principle: growing, maturing Christians are always exploring, reading, and learning. Study may include digging into Scripture through inductive Bible study or other helpful tools, reading books, or attending workshops, classes, and seminars. Listening to teachings from people ahead of you spiritually may also be included here. Consider studying not simply for information but for the purpose of formation in Christ. Pray back to God what you are learning. I love to read so I could easily have moved Study under the category of Rest. Yet I can think of a few friends who would move Study immediately to Work.

Sabbath

Develop a rhythm of setting apart one twenty-four-hour period each week. Most of us work a five-day week but need another day for doing the activities of life that are "work" for us. That might include paying bills, fixing your car, working on your house or apartment, finishing your homework if you are a student. Take some time to reflect on the four characteristics of biblical Sabbaths—stop, rest, delight, contemplate. What will it mean for you to stop and rest rather than use this as one more day to "get things done"? One key to my Sabbath is to purposely not think about New Life Fellowship Church, my place of work, nor look at e-mails or my answering machine. Waste time and don't look at the clock.

For those of us who work on Sundays, we need to carefully choose and stick with another day of the week. I choose Saturdays (in most weeks) because my children are off from school on that day. Yes, my commitment has a significant impact on them and what I am willing to do! Getting out of New York City to the beauty of nature is an important part of our Sabbaths.

Trust God to run the universe without you. Begin to look at your weeks as preparing for Sabbath! Ask yourself, "What kinds of activities bring me joy and delight? What truly replenishes me?" Take a nap. Enjoy God. Do something totally different from your work. Finally, when you plan your vacation this coming year, apply the principle of Sabbath. See it as an extended Sabbath to the Lord. Plan, in advance, how you will balance the four elements of biblical Sabbaths—stopping, resting, delighting, and contemplating—during that time.

Simplicity

The primary issue here is to remove distractions and remain free from attachments. "Live as free of complications as possible [so] you're free to concentrate on simply pleasing the Master" (1 Corinthians 7:32 MSG).

For this reason our children are not in three sports at one time while learning violin. We are careful to not buy every new electronic or technological item to help us save time. Instead of having five credit cards, we have one. Instead of cooking elaborate meals and having a house that is always perfectly clean, we have made choices to let that go. We are no longer involved in fifteen projects at the same time in our service for Christ. We do less, but do it better than before. We also got rid of our cable a number of years ago and opted for a DVD player instead.

The principle of tithing—that is, the giving away of 10 percent of our income—is also an important component to simplicity. It teaches us to let go of what is not necessary and to remain dependent on God as our security and source. Jesus himself taught that "where your treasure is, there your heart will be also" (Matthew 6:21). It is not a law as it was in the Old Testament, but it is a powerful principle that serves to keep us detached from the power of money. It also forces us to handle our money more carefully. We have been increasing our financial giving percentage each year as part of our Rule of Life and have seen God work miracle after miracle in providing for us. Get out of all unhealthy debt by attending a money-management seminar.

Play and Recreation

The key here is to engage in activities that are pure and healthy and that breathe life into you. Many Christians, in particular, are "fun deficient." We perhaps didn't grow up in families or environments that included play and recreation as a valid part of life. This requires planning and preparation. For example, many people, due to lack of planning, will watch a movie to relax, only to realize they feel worse spiritually, not better, when it is over.

Make no mistake: it is revolutionary to enjoy healthy pleasure. I believe this is a profound theological issue touching on how we view God, life, and creation. For this reason, each New Year's Eve our church hosts some sort of a non-alcoholic, intergenerational event that is fun! And I am convinced fun is one of Geri's spiritual gifts to the body of Christ. She summarizes part of her life mission as: "Life can be difficult, so have fun whenever you can to the glory of God." Remember

Ecclesiastes 3:4: there is "a time to weep and a time to laugh, a time to mourn and a time to dance."

Service and Mission

The question here is in what way(s) is God inviting me to serve him at this stage of my journey? In what way can I use my time, talents, resources, and gifts for others? What passions and desires has God placed within me? Every church and community has numerous opportunities to serve. This may also include volunteering to feed the homeless and hungry, looking for a person in a lonely social situation and finding ways to include her in your life, or mentoring a young person or new believer in Christ. Under this category I would include commitment to the poor and marginalized; to bridging racial, cultural, and economic barriers; to working for justice and the environment; to world missions. For some of us, our challenge is to do something for others outside of our comfort zone. For others like me, the issue is limits. How can I embrace my God-given limits and not go beyond what he is asking me to do?

Care for the Physical Body

Many of us take poor care of the bodies God has given us. Yet caring for our bodies can be as spiritual as prayer or worship. What might you want to include in your Rule of Life about exercise? How many times a week will you exercise? What will you do? What about your work habits? Are you eating a balanced, healthy, nutritious diet? What is the effect of certain foods on your energy level? Do you get adequate rest and sleep? Scripture says sleep is a gift of God (see Psalm 127:2). When is the last time you went to the doctor for an annual checkup?

What might be one area you want to include in your Rule of Life now? It may be that you want to begin to listen to your body and how God might be speaking to you through it. For example, a headache, knot in your stomach, inability to sleep, and the resulting exhaustion may be God calling you to slow down or to change directions. Listening to our bodies can be an important way to listen to God. When we care for our bodies, we acknowledge the holiness of all of life and honor the fact that God is within us.

Emotional Health

This has been part of my Rule of Life for the last eleven years. For a couple of years, it was as simple as paying attention to my feelings and journaling them to God a few times a week. Then I would ask God how he might be speaking to me through them.

It may be that you recognize you have a lot of unprocessed grief due to losses from your past. You may want to make that part of your plan over the next year. This may include reading, journaling, meeting with a trusted friend or counselor, or going on a personal "grief retreat." Part of your plan may include joining a small group that works through this book slowly. You may want to join a group that focuses on practical relational skills such as resolving conflict well or healthy communication practices.

Growth in understanding your sexuality, both as a single or married person, would come under this element. Geri and I continue to mature in this part of our Rule of Life. We read broadly and attend training events or courses that challenge us to grow in new ways. But like anything else, this, too, takes intentionality.

Family

This element applies both to people married and single. Marriage, parenting, and our relationship with our family of origin are all crucial discipleship issues. For example, what will I do this year to grow in parenting my four daughters, three of whom are now teenagers? What do I want them to learn before they transition into young adulthood? It is very easy for me to fall into passive patterns. What can I do to invest in our marriage this coming year? One of Geri's passions is the outdoors —hiking, camping, and enjoying the beauty of God's creation. I am content in a library or bookstore. While I enjoy our time outdoors together, it requires a plan to get me started.

Geri and I are best friends. We love our marriage. Yet we continue to search out opportunities, separately and together, to build into our relationship. If you are single, what is your plan to relate to your parents (or stepparents), your siblings? What kind of relationship would you like to have with them? What are one or two steps you can take to get there?

Community (Companions for the Journey)

Under this heading in your personal Rule of Life, you will want to ask yourself about the kind of companions you need for this next stage of your journey. If you are not part of a church, for example, you will want to ask God for direction and investigate places where you can both give and receive. What other support networks might you need inside or outside your local church? We recommend that everyone in our church connect relationally through a small group. Geri and I lead a small group in our home. We enjoy these relationships, but I am their pastor! So in my case, for example, I meet regularly with two of the elders of our church about my spiritual life. I also have a long-term mentor who is older and wiser in God. While he lives in another state, we exchange phone calls and occasional visits. I also see a spiritual director every month or two. This provides a time for peaceful listening with another, more-experienced person how God is moving in my life. Again, be open and be creative on how God might want you to walk this out during this season of your journey.

Reread or rethink your Rule of Life regularly. St. Augustine wanted his read once a week! Minimally, you will want to review and revisit your Rule of Life every year.

Again, begin slowly working on only one or two elements at a time. Be willing to make mistakes, try again, and learn new things. You may want to try sketching out a Rule of Life for a four-week period such as Advent or during Lent.

Remember, as Benedict wrote fifteen hundred years ago, "Your way of acting should be different from the world's way. The love of Christ must come before all else." Keep that before you and you won't go too far off.

BROADER APPLICATIONS OF A "RULE OF LIFE"

The focus of this chapter has been on the development and application of a Rule of Life for your personal, interior growth in God. That, for me, is one very clear application of a rich treasure in church history that is available to us today. The following are three other significant applications to consider for us as we enter the twenty-first century:

The Local Church

Every church has values, practices, and habits that they take for granted. Each is unique and has her way of doing things. People join a church and become part of her family. In some ways it is correct to say that every church has a Rule of Life. The problem is that it is often unconscious. The challenge is to identify and authenticate what that is and be clear about it. That definition provides boundaries for the church community in a way that provides safety and clarity. Then we can invite people to follow Christ under this particular broad Rule of Life. Broad categories for a church then might include:

- history and particular gifts of the local church (mission statement);
- worship;
- equipping;
- small groups and community;
- authority;
- Lord's Supper and baptism;
- hospitality;
- new members;
- the poor and marginalized;
- serving the larger community;
- emotional health; and
- world missions.

Then, within the broad Rule of our community, we invite each member to continually work on the specifics of their personal Rule of Life.

A Small Group or Task Group

A small group, for an agreed-upon period of time, may commit together to certain practices and habits to follow Christ. Task groups, such as worship teams or mission groups, will often agree on a certain Rule of Life as a group for following Christ—either orally or in writing.

The Family

A few people have been led to apply the development of a Rule of Life for their family. We have not done that, but I can see how the clarifying of what we do as a family could release great energy and focus. It sure sounds like a great idea!

LIVE FAITHFULLY THE LIFE GOD HAS GIVEN YOU

God has a different path for each of us.

My prayer as we close is that you would be faithful to yours. It is a tragedy to live someone else's life.

I know. I did it for years.

I would like to end our time together with a story from Carlo Caretto as he lived in North Africa among Muslims for ten years with the Little Brothers of Jesus community. He wrote that one day he was traveling by camel in the Sahara desert and came across about fifty men laboring in the hot sun to repair a road. When Carlo offered them water, to his surprise, he saw among them his friend Paul, another member of his Christian community.

Paul had been an engineer in Paris working on the atomic bomb for France. God had called him to leave everything and become a Little Brother in North Africa. At one point Paul's mother came asking Carlo for help understanding her son's life.

"I have made him an engineer," she said. "Why can't he work as an intellectual in the church? Wouldn't that be more useful?"

Paul was content to pray and to disappear for Christ in the Sahara desert.

Carlo then went on to ask himself: "What is my place in the great evangelizing work of the Church?" He answers his own question:

> My place was there—among the poor. Others would have the task of building, feeding, preaching. . . . The Lord asked me to be a poor man among the poor, a worker among workers. It is difficult to judge others . . . but the one truth we must cling desperately to is love.
>
> It is love that justifies our actions. Love must initiate all we do.
>
> If out of love Brother Paul has chosen to die on a desert road, then he is justified. If out of love . . . others build schools and hospitals, they are justified. If out of love . . . scholars spend their lives among books, they are justified. . . . The Lord asked me to be a poor man among the poor, a worker among workers. . . .
>
> I can only say, "Live love, let love invade you. It will never fail to teach you what you must do."[6]

In the same way, may God give you the courage to faithfully live your unique life in Christ. And may love invade you. It will never fail to teach you what you must do.

Lord, after reading this chapter, I just need to be with you—for a long time. I know that at other times I have rushed and cut you short, but I can see there are a lot of things in me that need to change. Let this time be different, Lord. Show me what one small step I can take to begin to build a life around you. Help me pay attention to your voice. By faith, I obey, trusting that even small changes will grow into powerful winds of the Holy Spirit blowing through and overtaking all of the areas of my life. Thank you. In Jesus' name, amen.

APPENDIX A

THE PRAYER OF EXAMEN
(AN ADAPTATION OF ST. IGNATIUS LOYOLA'S EXAMEN)

A classic spiritual practice developed by Ignatius Loyola (1491–1556) is called the "Prayer of Examen." It is a prayerful reflection of your experience with Jesus over a specific time period. The goal is simple: increased awareness and attentiveness to the presence of God in your daily life.

While it is normally done at the end of each day, it can be prayed at any time. Get in a comfortable position and still yourself. Recall you are in the presence of God, inviting the Holy Spirit to guide you as you review the events of your day. Walk through the events in your day (or yesterday's events if it is morning). Imagine yourself watching your day on a fast-forwarded DVD with Jesus. Let Jesus stop the DVD at any part of the day so you might reflect on it.

Notice those times when you were aware of God's presence, when you felt you were moving toward God. How did you feel when you were open and responsive to God's guidance? Give God thanks for those times.

Notice the times you were not aware of God's presence, when you felt you were moving away from God. What was blocking that awareness? Pray for forgiveness or healing, as appropriate, for those times.

End with prayer for grace to be more aware of God's presence. Close the time with a prayer of thanks for this time with God.

APPENDIX B

The following is a recent Daily Office I wrote as one possibility for people to use for their morning, midday, and evening prayer.

NEW LIFE FELLOWSHIP CHURCH: DAILY OFFICE (MARCH 2006)

Guidelines for the Daily Office

- An Office is a time to *stop*, *slow down*, *center*, and *pause* to be with Jesus. Our goal is to create a continual and easy familiarity with God's presence in each day.
- Start modestly, beginning with one Office before trying to do all of them regularly. Otherwise you risk getting discouraged and giving up entirely. Start slowly.
- Notice the silence at the beginning and conclusion of each Office. Consider being silent for thirty to forty-five seconds *between* the readings/prayers also. When silent, seek to sit still and straight. Breathe slowly, naturally, and deeply. Close your eyes, remaining present, open, and awake. Don't hurry! When you are alone, if God leads you to pause at a certain phrase or verse, stay with that. Less can be more.
- If you are doing an Office with others, agree on a leader to facilitate the pace. Also you may want to take turns reading/praying. Be sure to read the texts/prayers aloud (even if alone), slowly, prayerfully, and thoughtfully.

MORNING PRAYER

Silence and Centering (2–5 minutes)

"Be still before the LORD and wait patiently for him." (Psalm 37:7)

Opening Prayer

Though an army besiege me,
my heart will not fear;
though war break out against me,
even then will I be confident.
One thing I ask of the LORD,
this is what I seek:
that I may dwell in the house of the LORD
all the days of my life,
to gaze upon the beauty of the LORD
and to seek him in his temple.
For in the day of trouble
he will keep me safe in his dwelling. (Psalm 27:3–5)

Lord, help me this day to love you with all my heart and with all my soul and with all my mind and with all my strength, for this is the first and greatest commandment, and then to love my neighbor as myself. (See Matthew 22:37–39.)

New Testament Reading and Prayer

Heavenly Father, grant me the Spirit of wisdom and revelation that I may know you better. May the eyes of my heart be enlightened in order that I may know the hope to which you have called me. May I glimpse, by the Holy Spirit, the riches of your glorious inheritance in the saints and your incomparably great power for us who believe. May I experience that power today—the working of your mighty strength, which you exerted in Christ when you raised him from the dead and seated him at your right hand in the heavenly realms. (See Ephesians 1:17–20.)

Old Testament Reading (Ten Commandments—Exodus 20:1–17)

1. **YOU SHALL HAVE NO OTHER GODS BEFORE ME.**
   Lord, I detach myself from all things outside of you that compete for my ultimate affection.
2. **YOU SHALL NOT MAKE FOR YOURSELF AN IDOL**
   [i.e., another image for God].
   Help me not to shape you according to my own fears and ideas, but to trust and follow you, like Abraham, into the unknown.
3. **YOU SHALL NOT MISUSE THE NAME OF THE LORD YOUR GOD.**
   Enable me to represent you well in every conversation and interaction.
4. **REMEMBER THE SABBATH DAY BY KEEPING IT HOLY.**
   Prepare me that I may rest from all my works each day and set apart a day to put away all earthly anxieties to delight in you.
5. **HONOR YOUR FATHER AND YOUR MOTHER.**
   Help me to honor my parents appropriately. May I remember that the same way I treat them, I may be treated some day.
6. **YOU SHALL NOT MURDER.**
   May my interactions today with others, and my words, bring life and not death, edify and not tear down.
7. **YOU SHALL NOT COMMIT ADULTERY.**
   Free me to live purely, rightly, and respectfully to myself and others.
8. **YOU SHALL NOT STEAL.**
   Help me not to be greedy but to share joyfully with others.
9. **YOU SHALL NOT GIVE FALSE WITNESS.**
   Lord, help me to walk in the truth and to avoid false assumptions about other people and situations—not only in my own mind, but in my conversation with others.
10. **YOU SHALL NOT COVET.**
    May I love you above all else because "Your love is better than life."

Prayer for Others/Yourself

Optional Devotional Reading

Conclude with Silence (2–3 minutes)

MIDDAY PRAYER

Silence and Centering (2–5 minutes)

"Be still, and know that I am God." (Psalm 46:10)

Opening Prayer

Teach us to number our days aright, that we may gain a heart of wisdom. For a thousand years in your sight are like a day that has just gone by or like a watch in the night. . . . May the favor of the Lord our God rest upon us; establish the work of our hands, O Lord, establish the work of our hands. (See Psalm 90:14–17.)

We wait in hope for the LORD;
he is our help and our shield.
In him our hearts rejoice,
for we trust in his holy name.
May your unfailing love rest upon us, O LORD,
even as we put our hope in you. (Psalm 33:20–22)

Our Father in heaven,
hallowed be your name,
your kingdom come,
your will be done
on earth as it is in heaven.
Give us today our daily bread.
Forgive us our debts,
as we also have forgiven our debtors.
And lead us not into temptation,
but deliver us from the evil one.

For yours is the kingdom and the power and the glory forever. Amen. (See Matthew 6:9–13)

Concluding Prayer

Lord, you say that "in repentance and rest is [my] salvation, in quietness and trust is [my] strength." Teach me to rest and trust in you throughout the remainder of this day. "Teach me your way, O LORD, and I will walk in your truth; give me an undivided heart that I may fear your name. . . . For great is your love toward me." (Isaiah 30:15 and Psalm 86:11–13)

Conclude with Silence (2–3 minutes)

EVENING PRAYER

Silence and Centering (2–5 minutes)

When you are on your beds, search your hearts and be silent. (Psalm 4:4)

Opening Prayers

May my prayer be set before you like incense;
may the lifting up of my hands be like the evening sacrifice. (Psalm 141:2)

It is good to praise the LORD
and make music to your name, O Most High,
to proclaim your love in the morning
and your faithfulness at night. (Psalm 92:1–2)

I wait for the LORD, my soul waits,
and in his word I put my hope.
My soul waits for the Lord
more than watchmen wait for the morning,
more than watchmen wait for the morning.
O Israel, put your hope in the LORD,
for with the LORD is unfailing love. (Psalm 130:5–7)

New Testament Reading (Beatitudes)

BLESSED ARE THE POOR IN SPIRIT, FOR THEIRS IS THE KINGDOM OF HEAVEN. (MATTHEW 5:3)

God have mercy on me, a sinner. Help me accept my brokenness, emptiness, and need for you.

BLESSED ARE THOSE WHO MOURN, FOR THEY WILL BE COMFORTED. (5:4)

Lord, help me not to pretend but to embrace my vulnerability, humanity, and limits.

BLESSED ARE THE MEEK, FOR THEY WILL INHERIT THE EARTH. (5:5)

Lord, grant me grace to trust you and drop my defenses, be approachable, kind, merciful, and appropriately assertive.

BLESSED ARE THOSE WHO HUNGER AND THIRST FOR RIGHTEOUSNESS, FOR THEY WILL BE FILLED. (5:6)

Help me love you above all else. Purge my soul of all polluted affections, habits, and rebellions.

BLESSED ARE THE MERCIFUL, FOR THEY WILL BE SHOWN MERCY. (5:7)

Enable me to forgive as generously and consistently as you, Lord, forgive me.

BLESSED ARE THE PURE IN HEART, FOR THEY WILL SEE GOD. (5:8)

Lord, I ask for a pure (clean, uncluttered) heart. I long to see your face, that there would be nothing between you and me.

BLESSED ARE THE PEACEMAKERS, FOR THEY WILL BE CALLED SONS OF GOD. (5:9)

Lord, fill me with courage to disrupt false peace around me when needed. Give me wisdom and prudence to be a true peacemaker.

BLESSED ARE THOSE WHO ARE PERSECUTED BECAUSE OF RIGHTEOUSNESS, FOR THEIRS IS THE KINGDOM OF HEAVEN. (5:10)

Lord, fill me with courage to speak and live the truth, even when it is not popular or convenient.

Old Testament Reading

Have mercy on me, O God,
according to your unfailing love;
according to your great compassion
blot out my transgressions. . . .
Create in me a pure heart, O God,
and renew a steadfast spirit within me. . . .
Restore to me the joy of your salvation
and grant me a willing spirit, to sustain me. (Psalm 51:1, 10, 12)

Concluding Prayer

Almighty God, my heavenly Father: I have sinned against you, through my own fault, in thought, and word, and deed, in what I have done and what I have left undone. For the sake of your Son our Lord Jesus Christ, forgive me all my offenses; and grant that I may serve you in newness of life, to the glory of your Name. Amen. (Book of Common Prayer)

Prayer for Others/Yourself

Optional Devotional Reading

Final Prayer

May the Lord Almighty grant me and those I love a peaceful night and a perfect end. (Book of Common Prayer)

Conclude with Silence (2–3 minutes)

NOTES

INTRODUCTION

1. Peter Scazzero, *The Emotionally Healthy Church* (Grand Rapids: Zondervan, 2003).
2. Kieran Kavanaugh, ed., *John of the Cross: Selected Writings, Classics of Western Spirituality* (Mahwah, NJ: Paulist Press, 1987), 292.

CHAPTER 1

1. Alan Jamieson, *A Churchless Faith: Faith Journeys Beyond the Churches* (Great Britain: Society for Promoting Christian Knowledge, 2002).
2. For a more complete accounting of my story see chapters one and three of Pete Scazzero, *The Emotionally Healthy Church* (Grand Rapids: Zondervan, 2003).

CHAPTER 2

1. Bill Bright, "The Four Spiritual Laws" (New Life Publications, 1995), 12.
2. Thomas Merton, *Thoughts in Solitude* (Boston: Shambhala Publications, 1956), 13.
3. Quoted in Ron Sider, *The Scandal of the Evangelical Conscience: Why Are Christians Living Just Like the Rest of the World?* (Grand Rapids: Baker Books, 2005), 13.
4. Ibid., 17–27.
5. Ibid., 28–29.
6. Parker Palmer, *Let Your Life Speak: Listening for the Voice of Vocation* (San Francisco: Jossey-Bass, 2000), 30–31.
7. Quoted in Rowan Williams, *Where God Happens: Discovering Christ in One Another* (Boston: Shambhala Publications, 2005), 14.

CHAPTER 3

1. Richard Bauckham, *The Theology of the Book of Revelation* (Cambridge: Cambridge University Press, 1993). Preaching through the book of Revelation at New Life Fellowship in 2002–2003 transformed my understanding of the church, her calling and the demonic and cultural forces that confront the US. To order a sampling of these sermons go to www.emotionallyhealthychurch.com.
2. Os Guiness, *The Call: Finding and Fulfilling the Central Purpose of Your Life* (Nashville: Word Publishing, 1998), 57–58.
3. Martin Luther, *Commentary on Galatians* (Grand Rapids: Revell, 1994).
4. Defining and measuring emotional health or intelligence is a massive field with a wide range of opinions on what constitutes emotional maturity. Alongside my own reflections

I have gleaned from such sources as Lori Gordon, *PAIRS Semester Course*, PAIRS International, curriculum guide for trainers, 437; Joseph Ciarrochi, Joseph P. Forgas, and John Mayer, eds., *Emotional Intelligence in Everyday Life: A Scientific Inquiry* (New York: Psychology Press, 2001); and Cary Cherniss and Daniel Goleman, eds., *The Emotionally Intelligent Workplace: How to Select for, Measure, and Improve Emotional Intelligence in Individuals, Groups and Organizations* (San Francisco: Jossey-Bass, 2001). A very accessible secular resource is Cary Cherniss and Mitchel Adler, *Promoting Emotional Intelligence in Organizations: Make Training in Emotional Intelligence Effective* (Alexandria, VA: The American Society for Training and Development, 2000).

5. For a brief, but helpful description of the contemplative stream through church history, see Richard Foster, *Streams of Living Water: Celebrating the Great Traditions of Christian Faith*, (San Francisco: HarperSanFrancisco, 1998), 23–58. See also Tony Jones, *The Sacred Way: Spiritual Practices for Everyday Life* (Grand Rapids: Zondevan, 2005); Joan Chittister, *Wisdom Distilled from the Daily: Living the Rule of St. Benedict Today* (San Francisco: HarperSanFrancisco, 1990); Daniel Wolpert, *Creating a Life with God: The Call of Ancient Prayer Practices* (Nashville: Upper Room Books, 2003); and Robert E. Webber, *Ancient-Future Time: Forming Spirituality Through the Christian Year* (Grand Rapids: Baker Books, 2004).
6. I am thankful to Jay Feld for the initial diagram, which was then expanded into its present form.
7. Quoted in David W. Bebbington, *The Dominance of Evangelicalism: The Age of Spurgeon and Moody*, (Downers Grove, IL: InterVarsity Press, 2005), 35–40.
8. Thomas Merton. *New Seeds of Contemplation* (New York: New Directions, 1987), 14.
9. See chapter 8 entitled "Receive the Gift of Limits" in Scazzero, *The Emotionally Healthy Church*.
10. I was exposed to the notion of negative and positive scripts that we believe about ourselves through the work of Virginia Satir. One accessible work on her is: Sharon Loeschen, *The Satir Process: Practical Skills for Therapists* (Fountain Valley, California, 2002), 105–107; and Virginia Satir, *Your Many Faces: The First Step to Being Loved* (Berkeley, California: Celestial Arts, 1978), 25–26. I am also grateful for the rich insights and work found in, Lori Gordon, *PAIRS Semester Handbook: The Practical Application of Intimate Relationship Skills*, (Weston, FL: The PAIRS Foundation, 2003), 2–310.
11. Mark E. Thibodeaux, *Armchair Mystic: Easing Into Contemplative Prayer* (Cincinnati, OH: St. Anthony Messenger Press, 2001), chapter 2.
12. Brennan Manning, *Lion and Lamb: The Relentless Tenderness of Jesus* (Grand Rapids: Chosen Books, 1986), 24.
13. Thomas Merton, *The Wisdom of the Desert* (Boston: Shambhala Publications, 2004), 1–2, 25–26.

CHAPTER 4

1. See http://www.soul-guidance.com/houseofthesun/eckhart.htm.
2. John Calvin, *Institutes of the Christian Religion, Volume 1* (Grand Rapids: Eerdmans Publishing Company, 1957), 37.
3. Daniel Goleman, *Emotional Intelligence: Why It Can Matter More than IQ* (New York: Bantam Books, 1995), 199–200.
4. For a great introduction to Ignatius's teachings on discernment and our emotions, see

Thomas H. Green, *Weeds Among the Wheat: Discernment: Where Prayer and Action Meet* (Notre Dame: Ave Maria Press, 1984). See also the sermon series "Discovering the Will of God" available at www.emotionallyhealthychurch.com.

5. Dan Allender and Tremper Longman III, *The Cry of the Soul* (Dallas: Word, 1994), 24–25.
6. Quoted in James Finley, *Merton's Palace of Nowhere: A Search for God Through Awareness of the True Self* (Notre Dame: Ave Maria Press, 1978), 54.
7. M. Scott Peck, *A World Waiting to Be Born: Civility Rediscovered* (New York: Bantam Books, 1993), 112–113.
8. Richard Ben Cramer, *Joe DiMaggio: The Hero's Life* (New York: Simon and Schuster, 2000), 519.
9. *Leadership* (Summer 2002), 52–53.
10. M. Robert Mulholland Jr., *The Deeper Journey: The Spirituality of Discovering Your True Self* (Downers Grove, IL: InterVarsity Press, 2006). See chapters two and three for a detailed analysis of these consequences.
11. I am using the words *true self* in a way similar to M. Robert Mulholland Jr. (see previous endnote). In footnote 1 of chapter 2 in *The Deeper Journey*, Mulholland states: "Self is used here not in the contemporary sense of the psychological 'self,' an implicitly reductionistic term, but in the larger biblical sense of personhood framed within the context of a life lived in relationship with God, in community with others and as part of creation."
12. Michael Kerr and Murray Bowen, *Family Evaluation: The Role of the Family as an Emotional Unit That Governs Individual Behavior and Development* (New York: Norton Press, 1988), 97–109.
13. Merton, *New Seeds of Contemplation*, 35.
14. Parker Palmer, *A Hidden Wholeness: The Journey Toward an Undivided Life* (San Francisco: Jossey-Bass, 2004), 80–84.
15. Ibid., 114–115.
16. Benedicta Ward, trans., *The Sayings of the Desert Fathers* (Kalamazoo, MI: Cistercian Study Series, 1975), 139.
17. Dietrich Bonhoeffer, *Life Together* (New York: HarperCollins, 1954), 78.
18. Palmer, *A Hidden Wholeness*, 57.
19. John Cassian, *The Conferences*, trans. Boniface Ramsey (Mahwah, NJ: Paulist Press, 1997), 87–89.
20. Coleman Barks, trans., *The Illuminated Rumi* (New York: Doubleday, 1997), 80.
21. Bowen's material is summed up in Harriet Lerner, *The Dance of Anger: A Woman's Guide to Changing the Pattern of Intimate Relationships* (New York: Harper and Row, 1985), 34.
22. Chuck Yeager and Leo Janos, *Yeager: An Autobiography* (New York: Bantam Books, 1985), 154.
23. Ibid., 165.
24. Thomas Merton, *The Ascent to Truth* (New York: Harcourt Brace and Co., 1951), 238.

CHAPTER 5

1. See Judith Rich Harris, *The Nurture Assumption: Why Children Turn Out the Way They Do* (New York: Touchstone, 1998). The "nurture" proponents argue that what children learn in early years about relationships and rules for living life sets the pattern for the rest of their lives. The "nature" proponents look at genetic factors and biology. Judith Harris has argued that it is neither. Rather, she states that our peer groups of childhood and adoles-

cence shape our behavior and attitudes for life.

2. See Rodney Clapp, *Families at the Crossroads: Beyond Traditional and Modern Options* (Downers Grove, IL: InterVarsity Press, 1993) and Ray Anderson and Dennis Guernsey, *On Being Family: A Social Theology of the Family* (Grand Rapids: Eerdmans, 1985), 158.
3. For an excellent explanation and description of the five levels of the Beaver system of classifying families, see Maggie Scarf, *Intimate Worlds: Life Inside the Family* (New York: Random House, 1995).

CHAPTER 6

1. Janet O. Hagberg and Robert A. Guelich, *The Critical Journey: Stages in the Life of Faith.* (Salem, WI: Sheffield Publishing Company, 2005).
2. Ibid., 9.
3. Merton, *The Ascent to Truth*, 188–189.
4. For a concise, readable summary of God's goal for the destination of our journeys, see David G. Benner, *Sacred Companions: The Gift of Spiritual Friendship and Direction.* (Downers Grove, IL: InterVarsity Press, 2002). For a sermon series I preached on Journeying Through the Wall, go to www.emotionallyhealthychurch.com.
5. St. John of the Cross, *Dark Night of the Soul*, trans. E. Allison Peers (New York: Image, Doubleday Publishing), 1959.
6. Ibid., 36–90.
7. Gerald G. May. *The Dark Night of the Soul: A Psychiatrist Explores the Connection Between Darkness and Spiritual Growth* (New York: HarperCollins, 2004), 90.
8. St. John of the Cross, *The Dark Night of the Soul*, 106, 115.
9. This is the key teaching from James 1:3–4 when he writes about rejoicing in trials: "The testing of your faith develops perseverance. Perseverance must finish its work so that you may be mature and complete, not lacking anything." The Greek word translated "not lacking anything" carries with it the notion of God imparting or infusing something of his character into us through the process of difficulties and severe trials.
10. St. John of the Cross, *The Dark Night of the Soul*, 113, 117.
11. Karl Barth, *Church Dogmatics*, vol. 3, *The Doctrine of Reconciliation: Part One* (Edinburgh: T. & T. Clark, 1956), 231–234.
12. G. K. Chesterton, *St. Francis of Assisi* (New York: Image Books, Doubleday, 1957), 67.
13. Helen Bacovcin, trans., *The Way of a Pilgrim and The Pilgrim Continues His Way* (New York: Doubleday, 1978).
14. Merton, *The Ascent of Truth*.
15. Adapted from Robert Barron, *And Now I See: A Theology of Transformation* (New York: Crossroad Publishing, 1998), 148.
16. Wayne Muller, *Sabbath: Finding Rest, Renewal, and Delight in Our Busy Lives* (New York: Bantam, 1999), 187–188.
17. Everett Ferguson and Abraham J. Malherbe, trans., introduction and notes, *Gregory of Nyssa: The Life of Moses* (New York: Paulist Press, 1978), 94–97.
18. See G. K. Chesterton, *Saint Thomas Aquinas: "The Dumb Ox"* (New York: Image Books, Doubleday, 1956), 116, along with http://en.wikipedia.org/wiki/Thomas_Aquinas
19. Basil Pennington, *Thomas Merton, Brother Monk: The Quest for True Freedom* (New York: Continuum Publishing, 1997), 15–16.
20. Richard Rohr, *Adam's Return: The Five Promises of Male Initiation* (New York: Crossroad

Publishing, 2004).
21. Ibid., 152–166.
22. Merton, *New Seeds*, 203.

CHAPTER 7

1. John E. Hartley, *The Book of Job: The New International Commentary on the Old Testament* (Grand Rapids: Eerdmans, 1988), 82–83.
2. Froma Walsh and Monica McGoldrick, eds., *Living Beyond Loss: Death in the Family* (New York: W. W. Norton & Company, 1991), 105–106.
3. Gerald L. Sittser, *A Grace Disguised: How the Soul Grows Through Loss* (Grand Rapids: Zondervan, 1995), 33–34.
4. For a partial list, see James E. Loder, *The Logic of the Spirit: Human Development in Theological Perspective* (San Francisco: Jossey-Bass Publishers, 1998), 183–184.
5. Sheila Carney, "God Damn God: A Reflection on Expressing Anger in Prayer," *Biblical Theology Bulletin*, 13, no. 4 (October 1983), 116.
6. See Lori Gordon with Jon Frandsen, *Passage to Intimacy* (self-published, revised version, 2000), 40. I am grateful to PAIRS for this insight.
7. Robert Moore and Douglas Gillette, *King, Warrior, Magician, Lover: Rediscovering the Archetypes of the Mature Masculine* (San Francisco: HarperCollins, 1990), 23–47.
8. See Timothy Fry, ed., *RB 1980: The Rule of St. Benedict in English* (Collegeville, MN, 1981), 32–38.
9. For a fuller explanation of the distinction between a prayer life characterized by "Gimme, gimme, gimme" and a prayer life that is relational, see Larry Crabb, *The Papa Prayer: The Prayer You've Never Prayed* (Nashville: Integrity, 2006), 34–35.

CHAPTER 8

1. For an example, see http://www.lambtononline.com/winter_storms.
2. See the excellent book by Richard Swenson, *Margin: How to Create the Emotional, Physical, Financial, and Time Reserves You Need* (Colorado Springs: NavPress, 1992).
3. Countless good resources are available on spiritual disciplines. See Adele Ahlberg Calhoun, *Spiritual Disciplines Handbook: Practices That Transform Us* (Downers Grove, IL: InterVarsity Press, 2005); Tony Jones, *The Sacred Way: Spiritual Practices for Everyday Life* (Grand Rapids: Zondervan, 2005); and of course the classic by Richard Foster, *Celebration of Discipline* (New York: Harper and Row, 1986).
4. Robert Barron, *And Now I See*, 37. I am thankful to Barron for the insight that the core sin of the garden is the sin that leads us to take things into our own hands.
5. Ibid., 38.
6. James Loder, *The Logic of the Spirit: Human Development in Theological Perspective* (San Francisco: Jossey-Bass Publishers, 1998).
7. Phyllis Tickle, *The Divine Hours: Prayers for Autumn and Wintertime* (New York: Doubleday, 2000), xii.
8. Timothy Fry, *RB 1980*, 65.
9. A very readable and accessible three-volume series for the Daily Office is Phyllis Tickle, *The Divine Hours: Prayers for Autumn and Wintertime: A Manual for Prayer* (New York: Doubleday, 2001), *The Divine Hours: Prayers for Springtime: A Manual for Prayer* (New York: Doubleday, 2001), and *The Divine Hours: Prayers for Summertime: A Manual for Prayer* (New

York: Doubleday, 2000). I know many people who also use Norman Shawchuck and Rueben P. Job, *A Guide to Prayer for All Who Seek God* (Nashville: Upper Room Publishing, 2003) and The Northumbria Community, *Celtic Daily Prayer* (San Francisco: HarperCollins, 2002). I also like to follow along the readings of the psalms as laid out in the lectionary from the Book of Common Prayer.

10. James Finley, *Christian Meditation: Experiencing the Presence of God* (Great Britain: Society for Promoting Christian Knowledge, 2004), chapters 8–12.
11. Henri Nouwen, *Making All Things New* (San Francisco: Harper and Row, 1981), 69.
12. For a great introduction to other approaches you can integrate into your Daily Office, see Tony Jones, *The Sacred Way: Spiritual Practices for Everyday Life* (Grand Rapids: Zondervan, 2005).
13. This Daily Office is based on sermon series on both the Ten Commandments and the Beatitudes that I preached at New Life Fellowship Church. They are available at www.emotionallyhealthychurch.com.
14. For an excellent study on the word *holy*, see R. C. Sproul, *The Holiness of God* (Wheaton, IL: Tyndale House Publishers, 1985), 53–65.
15. This comes from Catholic theologian Leonard Doohan. It is quoted in an excellent book on Sabbath: Lynne M. Baab, *Sabbath Keeping: Finding Freedom in the Rhythms of Rest* (Downers Grove, IL: InterVarsity Press, 2005), 20.
16. Eugene Peterson, *Christ Plays in Ten Thousand Places: A Conversation in Spiritual Theology* (Grand Rapids: Eerdmans, 2005), 116–118.
17. Eugene Peterson, *Working the Angles: The Shape of Pastoral Integrity* (Grand Rapids: Eerdmans, 1987), 46.
18. Marva Dawn. *Keeping the Sabbath Wholly: Ceasing, Resting, Embracing, Feasting* (Grand Rapids: Eerdmans, 1989), 65–66.
19. Quoted in Wendell Berry, *Life Is a Miracle: An Essay Against Modern Superstition* (Washington, D.C: Counterpoint, 2000), 115.
20. Tilden Edwards, *Sabbath Time* (Nashville: Upper Room Books, 1992), 66.
21. Dr. Siang-Yang Tan, *Rest: Experiencing God's Peace in a Restless World* (Ann Arbor, MI: Servant Publications, 2000), 101–104.
22. I preached a four-part series on each of these components of biblical Sabbaths. They are available at www.emotionallyhealthychurch.com.
23. Every fifty years they were to take two years of Sabbath, adding to the one year a second called the Year of Jubilee (see Leviticus 25:8–55). Again, God knew the people would be afraid to take such a step of faith. So he promised he would provide enough harvest in the forty-ninth year so they could eat for three full years! Can you imagine?
24. Thomas Merton, *Conjectures of a Guilty Bystander* (New York: Doubleday, 1968), 86.

CHAPTER 9

1. *Sojourners* (July 2004), http:www.sojo.net/index.cfmaction-magazine.article&issue=sojo4070&article=040723.
2. See Robert Coleman, *The Master Plan of Evangelism* (Grand Rapids: Revell, 1963).
3. Merton, *Conjectures of a Guilty Bystander*, 156–158.
4. For a full description of emotional babies, children, adolescents, and adults, see Scazzero, *The Emotionally Healthy Church*, 66.
5. I first came across the phrase "practicing the presence of people" in Mike Mason,

Practicing the Presence of People: How We Learn to Love (Colorado Springs: WaterBrook Press, 1999).

6. Jean Vanier, *Becoming Human* (Mahwah, NJ: Paulist Press, 1998), 22.
7. M. Scott Peck, *A World Waiting to Be Born: Civility Rediscovered* (New York: Bantam Books, 1993), 108, 112.
8. Martin Buber, *I and Thou*, trans. Walter Kaufmann (New York: Charles Scribner's Sons, 1970).
9. Dante Alighieri, *The Divine Comedy*, vol. 1, trans. Mark Musa (New York: Penguin Books, 1984), 381.
10. C. S. Lewis, *The Great Divorce* (New York: Macmillan Company, 1946), 16–25.
11. Kenneth Paul Kramer with Mechthild Gawlick, *Martin Buber's I and Thou: Practicing Living Dialogue* (Mahwah, NJ: Paulist Press, 2003), 24.
12. Research has been done on how, when focusing attention away from negative behaviors and toward positive ones, people have been able to make permanent changes in their neural pathways. For an interesting study, see Jeffrey M. Schwartz and Sharon Begley, *The Mind and the Brain: Neuroplasticity and the Power of Mental Force* (New York: Regan Books, HarperCollins, 2002).
13. Pat Ennis, *The Third Option: Ministry to Hurting Marriages*, Topic #1, "Respect," 1–17.
14. I learned this tool from Lori Gordon, *PAIRS: Semester Course Handbook* (Weston, FL: PAIRS Foundation, 2003).
15. Pat Ennis, *The Third Option: Ministry to Hurting Marriages*, Teachers Manual, Topic #3, "Expectations," 1–9.
16. Lori Gordon with Jon Frandsen, *Passage to Intimacy*, 245,246.

CHAPTER 10

1. Jane Tomaine, *St. Benedict's Toolbox: The Nuts and Bolts of Everyday Benedictine Living* (Harrisburg: Morehouse Publishing, 2005), 5.
2. Catherine Doherty, *Poustinia: Encountering God in Silence, Solitude and Prayer* (Ontario, Canada: Madonna House Publications, 1993), 70.
3. Fry, *Rule of St. Benedict*, prologue, 45, 48–49.
4. Dallas Willard, *The Spirit of the Disciplines: Understanding How God Changes Lives* (San Francisco: HarperCollins, 1988), 63.
5. See Daniel Wolpert, *Creating a Life with God: The Call of Ancient Prayer Practices* (Nashville: Upper Room Books, 2003), 138–147.
6. Carlo Caretto, *Letters from the Desert*, anniversary edition (Maryknoll, NY: Orbis Books, 1972, 2002), 108, 100, 23.

EMOTIONALLY HEALTHY SPIRITUALITY WORKBOOK

ISBN: 1-59145-546-4

THOMAS NELSON
Since 1798